More

In-Depth Discussion of the Reasoning Activities
in
"Teaching Fractions and Ratios
for
Understanding"

More

In-Depth Discussion of the Reasoning Activities in "Teaching Fractions and Ratios for Understanding"

Susan J. Lamon
Marquette University

LAWRENCE ERLBAUM ASSOCIATES, PUBLISHERS

1999   Mahwah, New Jersey   London

ISBN 0-8058-3299-8
Printed in the United States of America

To Mrs. Hancock's fifth graders
For all that you taught me

Contents

Part I
Discussion of Activities

Chapter 1
Proportional Reasoning: An Overview

1. If 6 men can build a house in 3 days, then to shorten the time, you will need more men on the job. As the number of men goes up, the number of days goes down. If they are all working at the same rate, then each man does $\frac{1}{18}$ of the job each day. It would take 18 men to complete the house in 1 day. It would take 3 times as many men to complete the job in $\frac{1}{3}$ the time.

2. In each share, boy A gets 2 candies and boy B gets 3 candies. It takes 5 candies to give each boy one share. If you have 80 candies, you can give out 16 shares. In 16 shares, boy A gets 32 candies and boy B gets 48 candies.

3. If 5 chocolates cost $.75, then 10 cost $1.50 and 1 costs $.15, so 3 cost $.45. The cost of 13 candies (10 + 3) is $1.50 + $.45 or $1.95.

4. This problem is like problem 2. John has 3 times as many marbles as Mark, so you can think of the whole set of marbles being divided into 4 groups. John has 3 groups and Mark has 1 group. Because there are 32 marbles, there are 8 marbles in each group. John has 24 marbles and Mark has 8.

5. This problem is like problem 3. To read 14 chapters, it will take Jane 14 times as long as it takes her to read 1 chapter. It will take her 14 x 30 minutes or 7 hours.

6. This problem is like problem 1. The more people you have working, the faster the job will get done (assuming, of course, that the boys do not goof off on the job). If 6 boys were given 20 minutes to clean up, then 1 boy should be given 120 minutes, and 9 should be given $\frac{40}{3}$ or $13\frac{1}{3}$ minutes.

7. No answer. Knowing the weight of one player is no help in determining the weight of 11 players. People's weights are not related to each other.

8. This problem is like problems 2 and 4. Every time they put away $7, Sandra pays $2 and her mom pays $5. To get $210, they will need to make their respective contributions 30 times. In all, Sandra will contribute $60 and her mom will contribute $150.

9. If you decrease the number of people doing a job, it will take longer to get the job finished. If you have $\frac{1}{3}$ the number of people working, then it will take them 3 times as long to get the job done. It will take 288 minutes or 4 hours and 48 minutes.

10. This problem is like problems 3 and 5. For each $.30, the bike will run for 10 minutes. On $.90 worth of fuel, it will run for 30 minutes. On the remaining $.15 worth of fuel, it will run for 5 minutes. For $1.05, you could drive the bike for 35 minutes.

11. Your shadow (8') is 1.6 times as tall as you are (5'), so the shadow cast by the telephone pole must be 1.6 times as tall as the pole. If the shadow is 48 feet and that is 1.6 times the real height of the telephone pole, the pole must be 30' tall. Also, the telephone pole's shadow is 6 times as long as yours, so it must be 6 times as tall as you are.

12. In a square, two adjacent sides have the same length. That means that the ratio of the measure of 1 side to the measure of the other side would be 1. The rectangle that is most square is the one whose ratio of width to length is closest to 1. For the 35" x 39" rectangle, the ratio is $\frac{35}{39}$ or about .90. For the 22" x 25" rectangle, the ratio is $\frac{22}{25}$ or .88. This means that the 35" x 39" rectangle is most square.

13. Gear A has 1.5 times the number of teeth on gear B. So every time A turns once, B turns 1.5 times. If A makes 5.5 revolutions, B makes 5.5 (1.5) or 8.25 revolutions.

14. The density or crowdedness of a town with cars is given by comparing the number of cars to the number of square miles in the town. For town A, the crowdedness is $\frac{12555}{15}=837\frac{\text{cars}}{\text{sq.mi.}}$ For town B, it is $\frac{2502}{3}=834\frac{\text{cars}}{\text{sq.mi.}}$ For town C, it is $\frac{14212}{17}=836\frac{\text{cars}}{\text{sq.mi.}}$ The town least crowded with cars is town B. B must be Birmingham.

15. Several different approaches are given:
a. In pitcher A, 4 out of 7 total cubes are cranberry; in B, 3 out of 5 total cubes are cranberry. Because $\frac{3}{5}>\frac{4}{7}$, B has a stronger cranberry taste.
b. In pitcher A, the ratio of cranberry to apple is 4 to 3; in B, the ratio of cranberry to apple is 3 to 2. Because $\frac{3}{2}>\frac{4}{3}$, B has a stronger cranberry taste.
c. Using common denominators, pitcher A has 4 of the 7 total cubes or

$\frac{4}{7} = \frac{20}{35}$ cranberry; B has $\frac{3}{5}$ of is total cubes or $\frac{3}{5} = \frac{21}{35}$ cranberry. So B has a stronger cranberry taste.

d.   Using common denominators in comparing ratios within each pitcher, $\frac{3}{2} = \frac{9}{6} > \frac{4}{3} = \frac{8}{6}$, so B has a stronger cranberry taste.

16.   In a true enlargement, all dimensions grow by the same factor. Suppose the original picture measured 5 cm. x 6.5 cm.. If the picture were enlarged and the width increased from 5 to 9, it grew to 1.8 times its original width, and the new length should also be 1.8 times the original length, or 11.7 cm. This means that the 9 cm. x 10 cm. picture is not its enlargement. Check each pair of pictures to find the cases where the length and width were both multiplied by the same factor in going from the smaller to the larger picture. You will find that picture B is an enlargement of picture C. Both dimensions of C are multiplied by 1.25.

17.   There are several different ways in which this task could be accomplished. Here are four possibilities:
a. All 6 cats are needed to kill a rat. They polish him off in one minute, while the other rats stand by and wait their turn.
b. Three cats are needed to kill a rat and they do it in 2 minutes.
c. Two cats kill a single rat, and they do it in 3 minutes.
d. Each cat kills a rat single-handedly and takes 6 minutes to do it.

If you assume that the rats are dumb enough to stand by and wait their turn, that there is some orderly way of assigning the rats to each of the cats, and agree to disregard the foolishness of fractional cats and rats, here are some solutions:
(i) If 6 cats together kill 1 rat in 1 minute, then it would take 12 cats to kill 2 rats in 1 minute. So if the 12 have 50 times as long to do it, they can kill 50 times as many rats (100 rats).
(ii) If 3 cats kill 1 rat in 2 minutes, then 12 cats (4 times as many cats) could kill 4 rats (4 times as many rats) in 2 minutes. The same 12 cats could kill 25 times as many rats if they have 25 times as long to do it. So they could kill 100 rats in 50 minutes.
(iii)   6 cats / 1 rat / 1 minute
        6 cats / 300 rats / 300 minutes
        2 cats / 100 rats / 300 minutes
       12 cats / 100 rats / 50 minutes

18.   When weights are placed farther from the fulcrum, they will exert a greater effect or downward pull. Weights closer to the fulcrum have a lesser effect. A heavier weight closer to the center may be counteracted by a smaller weight placed farther out. So how much "tipping" you get depends on the amount of weight you have put on each side and how far along the arm each weight is placed. In A, there are 3 weights on the left side, each 3 units from the fulcrum or 3(3) = 9 units of pull. On the

right side, there are 2 weights, each 4 units from the fulcrum or 2(4) = 8 units of pull. The balance will tip to the left. In B, you have 1(4) + 2(3) + 1(2) = 12 units of pull on the left , and 1(4) + 2(2) + 1(1) = 9 units of pull on the right. Again, the beam will tip to the left. Also notice that in B, the far weights balance, while the closer weights are farther to the left.

19. A picture may be the best way to represent this situation. Shade $\frac{2}{3}$ of a rectangle to represent the married men and $\frac{3}{4}$ of another rectangle to represent the married women. Because the corresponding numbers of men and women are equal, position the rectangles so that the shaded parts overlap.

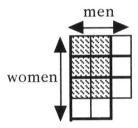

Then you can clearly see that the total number of women is the same as $\frac{8}{9}$ of the total number of men. The ratio of men to women is 9:8.

20. Let A be the coffee sold for $8 per pound, and B, the coffee sold for $14 per pound. If we buy A alone, we pay $8 per pound. If equal amounts of each type of coffee are used in the mixture (25 lb. of A and 25 lb. of B), then we will pay $11 per pound. There must be more of A because the mixture is selling for $10 per pound.

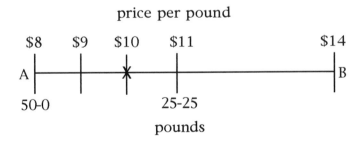

Because the cost of the mixture is $\frac{2}{3}$ of the way between $8 and $11, the amount of A must be $\frac{1}{3}$ of the way between 25 and 50 pounds. There are $33\frac{1}{3}$ pounds of coffee A, and the rest of the mixture ($16\frac{2}{3}$ pounds) must be coffee B.

Chapter 2
Relative and Absolute Thinking

1. Both the King family and the Jones family have two girls. However, the families have different numbers of children, so that if we think about the number of girls as compared to (or relative to) the number of boys or to the total number of children, then the situation looks different in each family. If we compare the number of girls to the total number of children, in the Jones family $\frac{2}{5}$ of the children are girls and in the King family, $\frac{2}{4}$ or $\frac{1}{2}$ of the children are girls. The ratio of girls to boys in the Jones family is 2:3, while in the King family, it is 2:2. Therefore, we would say that the King family has a greater proportion of girls or that more of the King family is girls.

2. Merely by counting the brown eggs in each container, we can tell that the 18-egg container has more brown eggs. However, we might consider the fact that the containers hold different numbers of eggs. 7 out of the 18 eggs or $\frac{7}{18}$ are brown. 4 out of the 12 eggs or $\frac{1}{3}$ of the dozen are brown. Because $\frac{7}{18}$ is more than $\frac{1}{3}$, the dozen-and-a half container has more brown eggs in both an absolute and in a comparative sense. This problem shows the importance of asking students to explain their reasoning. If a student said that the larger container has more brown eggs, we would not know if the student was or was not thinking relatively.

3. The answer to "how much" is n o t a number of slices. Pan B contains $\frac{3}{8}$ of a pizza more than pan A contains. You could serve up the amount of pizza in A $2\frac{1}{2}$ times out of the pizza in B. Note that these comparisons are OK in this situation because the pizzas are the same size. If they were not, these questions would not be meaningful.

4. To decide which ramp is steeper, you cannot merely measure the part on which you ski. How steep something is depends on how the amount it goes up is spread over a horizontal distance. For example, it you walk up a vertical distance of 1200 feet but do it gradually, say, over the distance of 2 miles, you will not feel that you have been traveling a steep road. But if you rise 1200 feet in the course of half a mile, you would be walking a very steep path! So steepness is a comparison of how high you rise to the horizontal distance it takes to rise that distance. You

would need to know the measurements of the bases of each of the ramps and then compare $\dfrac{7}{m(\text{base A})}$ and $\dfrac{10}{m(\text{base B})}$ to see which is steeper.

5. You can tell who walked farther merely by adding the distances that each person walked. Dan walked 6 miles and Tasha walked 7 miles.

6. To decide who walked faster, you have to do more than merely find total distances. Speed requires that you compare the distance to the time it took to walk it. Dan traveled his 6 miles in 2.5 hours, so his speed was $\dfrac{6 \text{ mi.}}{2.5 \text{ hr.}} = \dfrac{2.4 \text{ mi.}}{\text{hr.}}$. Tasha walked her 7 miles in the same amount of time, so her speed was $\dfrac{7 \text{ mi.}}{2.5 \text{ hr.}} = \dfrac{2.8 \text{ mi.}}{\text{hr.}}$.

7. It is more helpful to know the percent of discount because then you know the amount you can save on an item of any price. 20% means that you will save $.20 for every dollar that you spend. If someone tells you only a dollar amount, you cannot tell if it is a good sale or not. $2.00 off on an item whose original cost was $500 is hardly worth the effort of rushing down to the store, but a savings of $2.00 on a $5.00 item is a substantial savings.

8. To judge the crowdedness of an elevator, you need to know how many people are on the elevator; however, that it not enough information. You might not call it crowded if there are ten people on an elevator that holds 25 people, but if there are 10 people on an elevator that holds 8, things are tighter! The number of people on the elevator must be compared to the recommended capacity or to the floor area (the number of square feet of floor space) in order to be able to tell if the elevator is crowded or not.

9. What does it mean to be square? In a square, two adjacent sides have the same length, so if you compared them, you would get a ratio of 1:1. Find the ratios of adjacent sides in each of the rectangles and see how close they are to 1. The ratio of adjacent sides for the 75' x 114' rectangle is $\dfrac{75}{114}$ or .66. The ratio of adjacent sides for the 455' x 494' rectangle is $\dfrac{455}{494}$ or .92. The ratio for the 284' x 245' rectangle is $\dfrac{245}{284}$ or .86. The 455' x 494' rectangle is most square.

10. Fred is not thinking relatively in this situation! Fewer pieces does not mean less pizza. The size of the pieces is a comparison of the total size of the pizza to the number of pieces (assuming that those pieces are cut the same size). Cutting a pizza into fewer pieces means that each slice will be bigger; it will contain a larger amount of the pizza's total area.

11. Ty doesn't understand the inverse relationship between the number of parts and the size of the parts. You might get him to think about it by asking, "Your Mom has 2 identical cherry pies. She cuts one into 9 equal pieces and the other into 5 equal pieces. You really like her cherry pie. From which pie do you want to have your piece?"

12. Neither boy understands that when you consider the full number of equal-sized pieces in a unit, you have a whole unit. In one whole unit, it does not matter how many pieces there are or what size they are. The relationship between number of pieces and size of pieces is relevant only when you are considering fractional parts of a unit.

Chapter 3
Fractions and Rational Numbers

1. One example is a combination problem: Joe's ice cream store sells three different flavors of ice cream, a choice of large or small cone or dish, and four different toppings. How many different purchases can you make at Joe's?

A second example is an area problem: A rectangle is 5 cm. long and 3 cm. wide. What is its area?

Another common type is a multiplicative comparison problem: Last month, Jack collected money from 135 customers on his paper route. This month, he collected from $\frac{3}{5}$ as many as last month. How many customers paid their bills this month?

2. A common example is a speed problem: If Mrs. Jones traveled 145 miles in $2\frac{1}{2}$ hours, what was her average speed for her trip? When you divide miles by hours, you get miles per hour.

3. Here is an example: For a project he is doing, Mr. Carter needs 15 pieces of rope each $\frac{3}{8}$ of a meter long . He has 5 meters of rope in the garage. How many pieces can he cut from the rope he has before he needs to buy more?

4. Here is one example: If a yard of material costs $3.95, how much will $\frac{3}{8}$ of a yard cost?

5. $.44 per 88 grams means $\frac{44 \text{ cents}}{88 \text{ grams}}$ or $\frac{\$.44}{88 \text{ grams}} = \frac{\$.01}{2 \text{ grams}}$. This says 1 cent per 2 grams. Another way to read it is to separate the fractional number from the label: $\frac{1}{2} \frac{\text{cent}}{\text{gram}}$. This is one-half cent per gram.

6. This is a division problem. To obtain a rate of travel, you compare how much distance has been traveled to the time it took to travel. 4 miles in 15 minutes can be written in several ways: $\frac{4 \text{ mi.}}{15 \text{ min.}} = \frac{1 \text{ mi.}}{3.75 \text{ min.}}$ (4 miles per 15 minutes is the same rate as 1 mile per 3.75 minutes). Another way is $\frac{4 \text{ mi.}}{15 \text{ min.}} = \frac{16 \text{ mi.}}{1 \text{ hr.}}$ (4 miles per 15 minutes is the same rate as 16 miles per 1 hour.)

7. Some possible answers include price = cost per item and density = number per area.

8. Although you see three different models, a set model, an area model, and a number line model, all three figures represent the same relative amount, $\frac{2}{3}$. In each case, 2 out of 3 equal parts are shown.

9. The first picture below shows $\frac{1}{4}$ of a 2-unit. That is, $\frac{1}{4}$ of 2 things considered as a unit. The second picture shows $\frac{2}{4}$ of 1 unit, or $\frac{2}{4}$ of a single, simple unit. If the items that are used to form the 2-unit and the 1-unit are identical, then the result *looks* the same. However, because you had a different unit in each case, the fraction used to name each result is different. In the first case, the result is $\frac{1}{4}$, and in the second case, the result is $\frac{2}{4}$ or $\frac{1}{2}$.

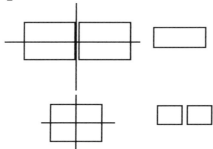

Chapter 4
Units and Unitizing

Remember: Many of the solutions are meant to be suggestive, not exhaustive!

1.a. If $\frac{1}{3}$ is 4 squares, then $\frac{3}{3} = 1$ must be 12 squares.

b. If 3 spaces is $\frac{3}{4}$, then 1 space is $\frac{1}{4}$, so $\frac{4}{4} = 1$ must be 4 spaces.

c. If $1\frac{1}{2}$ or $\frac{3}{2}$ is 12 dots, then $\frac{1}{2}$ must be 4 dots and $\frac{2}{2} = 1$ must be 8 dots.

Note that this problem can be solved visually. Each row represents $\frac{1}{2}$.

2. a. Because 4 dobs -3 dobs is 3 squares, 1 dob must be 3 squares. So 2 dobs + 1 dob must be 6 squares + 3 squares = 9 squares.

b. Because 7 teps - 5 teps is 3 squares, 2 teps = 3 squares. 6 teps - 2 teps must be 9 squares - 3 squares = 6 squares.

c. If $3\frac{2}{3} = \frac{11}{3}$ is 11 small rectangles, then $\frac{1}{3}$ is 1 small rectangle. 4 small rectangles must be $\frac{4}{3}$ or $1\frac{1}{3}$.

d. If $\frac{3}{7}$ is 9 triangles, then $\frac{1}{7}$ is 3 triangles, so $\frac{5}{7}$ must be 15 triangles.

3. The three slices of turkey Jake bought were $\frac{1}{3}$ of a pound. In order to determine how much $\frac{1}{4}$ pound is, you must first know what the unit is. If 3 slices = $\frac{1}{3}$ pound, then 9 slices = 1 pound. If 1 pound or $\frac{4}{4}$ = 9 slices, then $\frac{1}{4}$ pound must be $2\frac{1}{4}$ slices.

4. Unitizing does not change the unit. Unitizing merely chunks the unit into pieces of various sizes.

5. Hopefully, you would not use this poster if your students were recently introduced to the meaning of part—whole fractions. The same unit should be used to represent each fraction in a side-by-side

representation so that the sizes of the fractions relative to each other are accurately portrayed. Because the unit is different for each fraction, a child could draw some inappropriate conclusions (e.g., $\frac{1}{2}$ and $\frac{1}{5}$ are equivalent because the same number of equal parts are shaded for both and that $\frac{2}{3}$ and $\frac{2}{4}$ are equivalent because the same number of equal parts are shaded for both.)

6. Amy thought of the package of cupcakes as a single composite unit, that is, as 1(3-unit). She cut that one package into four equal parts. Seth thought of the package of cupcakes as 3(1-unit)s, that is, as 3 individual cupcakes. He cut each cupcake into four equal pieces.

7. Ed's solution shows that he gave each person $1(\frac{2}{3}\text{-bar})$. Brian first distributed half bars and then split the remaining two halves into sixths. Brian gave each person $1(\frac{1}{2}\text{-bar}) + 1(\frac{1}{6}\text{-bar})$.

8. a. $5(\text{6-packs}) = 2\frac{1}{2}(\text{12-packs}) = 1\frac{1}{4}(\text{24-packs})$
b. $2\frac{4}{5}(\text{5-packs}) = \frac{14}{18}(\text{18-pack})$
c. 2(24-packs)
d. 11 pair

9. Many answers are possible. Here are just a few. We give the name "triplets" to 1(3-group) of identical children. A "score" is 1(20-group). A "quartet" is 1(4-group) of instruments or voices.

10. $\frac{1}{3}\text{rec} = \frac{2}{3}\text{block}$ = 1 railroad track = 2 longs = 4 sticks = 8 mini-longs = 24 mini-blocks = 12 mini-sticks = 4 mini-recs

11. For some parts, many answers are possible.
a. $\frac{2}{3}$
b. 17 sticks
c. 36
d. 7 mini-recs
e. $\frac{1}{3}$
f. $1\frac{1}{2}$
g. 7 mini-sticks

12. It is important not to give students the impression that they can generate new names for every answer. When we divide area by area,

the result it not area. It is the number of times the divisor (an area) covers the dividend (another area). Students should be encouraged to think about the meaning of the operations being performed and about the meaning of the results.

13. Many questions are possible. Here are a few. Questions refer to Rec 2.

1 rec = _____ blocks   Answer $1\frac{5}{9}$ blocks

2 recs = _____ railroad tracks   Answer $2\frac{1}{3}$ railroad tracks

1 rec = _____ longs   Answer $4\frac{2}{3}$ longs

14. Yes. Each child received $\frac{1}{6}$ of the cake.

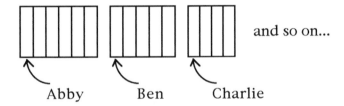

and so on...

Abby   Ben   Charlie

Chapter 5
Part-Whole Comparisons

1. a. The triangles are 4 of the 9 items in the group: $\frac{4}{9}$

b. The unit is the entire group of figures.

c. Two triangles are half the set of four triangles: $\frac{2}{4} = \frac{1}{2}$

d. In this case, the question makes it clear that the unit is the set of triangles, not the entire set of figures.

e. Three circles compared to the number of circles in the set is $\frac{3}{5}$.

f. The set of 5 circles is explicitly named as the unit.

2. The unit is the number of dogs. They can be counted; however, in this problem, we are given a way to compare the set of cats to the set of dogs without actually assigning a measure and quantifying them. We are told the way the number of cats compares to the number of dogs and so we do not need to know the exact numbers. Whatever the number of dogs is, the number of cats is $\frac{2}{3}$ of that number. The number of cats is smaller and we can show the comparison by letting a rectangle represent the number of dogs. If we take the set of dogs and divide it into 3 equal groups, the number of cats will be the same as the number of dogs in two of those groups.

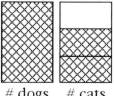

dogs   # cats

3. Compare 4 couples to the 12 people in a row by reunitizing a) the 12 people as couples, or b) the couples as single people.

$$\frac{4 \text{ couples}}{6 \text{ couples}} = \frac{8 \text{ people}}{12 \text{ people}}$$

Note that $\frac{4 \text{ couples}}{1 \text{ row}}$ is not a valid part—whole comparison because both sets are not unitized in the same way.

$$\frac{4 \text{ couples}}{6 \text{ couples}} = \frac{8 \text{ people}}{12 \text{ people}} = \frac{2 \text{ quads}}{3 \text{ quads}}$$

4. The band is $\frac{5}{8}$ girls and $\frac{3}{8}$ boys. With 12 more boys, the numbers of girls and boys are the same, so 12 students must be $\frac{2}{8}$ of the band. This means that $\frac{1}{4}$ of the band is 12 students and the whole band is composed of 48 students, 30 girls and 18 boys.

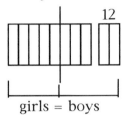

girls = boys

5. a. $\dfrac{3 \text{ days}}{5 \text{ days}}$

b. $\dfrac{12 \text{ pair}}{1 \text{ pair}}$

c. $\dfrac{1 \text{ pair}}{12 \text{ pair}}$

d. $\dfrac{\frac{8}{12} \text{ (12-pack)}}{1(12\text{-pack})}$

e. $\dfrac{1\frac{1}{3}(6\text{-packs})}{1(6\text{-pack})}$

f. $\dfrac{1\frac{1}{2}(\text{half dollars})}{1(\text{half dollar})}$

g. $\dfrac{4\frac{1}{4} \text{ acres}}{1 \text{ acre}}$

h. $\dfrac{8\frac{1}{2}(\frac{1}{2}\text{-acres})}{1(\frac{1}{2}\text{-acres})}$

6. a. 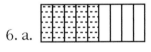 The portion of the committee composed of women.

b.

c.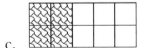

d.  $\frac{1}{6}$ of the cake is left.

e. 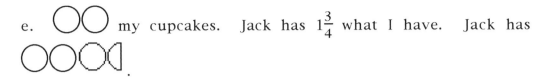 my cupcakes.   Jack has $1\frac{3}{4}$ what I have.   Jack has

7. The area of the square is A = s^2 or 25 sq. ft.   The area of the circle is A = $\pi \cdot r^2$ or 12.57 sq. ft.   The part of the square covered by the circle is $\frac{12.57}{25}$ or just a little over half the square.

8. This child has made a correct drawing of each of the fractions $\frac{4}{5}$ and $\frac{5}{6}$. The problem is that she cannot draw it accurately enough to be able to detect the difference in area between $\frac{1}{5}$ and $\frac{1}{6}$. One of the dangers of using an area model is that it is effective for comparing fractions only to the extent that children can make equal-sized pieces and the fractions are not too close in size to visually detect any difference.   The model should not be used when it may lead the child to wrong conclusions.   The child whose work we see here was severely misled.   It appears that one wrong conclusion supported another misconception. The child's conclusion that the remaining pieces were the same size reinforced the misconception that the fractions were the same size because they were each one piece away from the whole.

An acre is $5(\frac{1}{5}$-acres$)$ or $10(\frac{1}{10}$-acres$)$ or $30(\frac{1}{30}$-acres$)$.

9. a. Look at the columns. $\frac{2}{3}$ is 12 spots.

b. Look at the rows. $\frac{5}{6}$ is 15 spots.

c. Look at each vertical pair, like this: 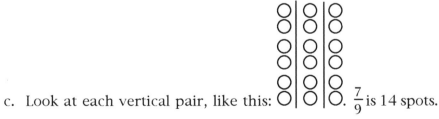 $\frac{7}{9}$ is 14 spots.

d. Imagine the second column of spots cut in half like this

then each spot and a half is $\frac{1}{12}$. $\frac{7}{12}$ is $10\frac{1}{2}$ spots.

e. Look at individual spots. $\frac{11}{18}$ is 11 spots.

10. Note that in this problem, the unit is the set of 18 hearts. Think about what each fraction means in relation to that unit.

$$\frac{5}{6} = \frac{5(3\text{-packs})}{6(3\text{-packs})} = \frac{15 \text{ hearts}}{18 \text{ hearts}}$$

$$\frac{2}{3} = \frac{2(6\text{-packs})}{3(6\text{-packs})} = 12 \text{ hearts out of the 18}$$

$$\frac{5}{9} = \frac{5(2\text{-packs})}{9(2\text{-packs})} = 10 \text{ hearts out of the 18}$$

$\frac{5}{9}$ is smallest.

Chapter 6
Partitioning and Quotients

1. Imagine cutting the first two objects in half and the third object into fourths.

2. Imagine giving each person 2 objects and then cutting the fifth object in half.

3. Imagine giving each person 4 rectangles or 2 columns.

4. Imagine giving each person 2 squares or 1 column.

5. Imagine giving each person 2 rows.

6. Imagine giving each person 1 row and 1 small square and $\frac{1}{3}$ of 1 square.

7. Imagine giving each person 1 entire piece and 1 small square.

8. Look at it this way

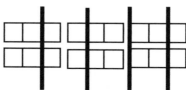

and then each person will get 4 squares and a half of a square.

9. a. If 4 people share 6 candy bars, how much candy will each receive? $\frac{6}{4}$ or $\frac{3}{2}$ of a candy bar.

b. If 4 people share 6 candy bars, how much of the candy does each receive? $\frac{1}{4}$ of the candy

10. e

11. b

12. d

13. b

14. The children all proposed to give each person $1\frac{1}{3}$ candy bars, but they also proposed different ways of breaking the candy bars. In each case, one share of the candy looks different and is named by different fractions:

$$\frac{1}{3}+\frac{1}{3}+\frac{1}{3}+\frac{1}{3}$$

$$\frac{1}{2}+\frac{1}{2}+\frac{2}{6}$$

$$\frac{1}{2}+\frac{1}{2}+\frac{1}{3}$$

$$\frac{2}{6}+\frac{2}{6}+\frac{2}{6}+\frac{2}{6}$$

Based on these partitions, the following fractions must be equivalent:

$$\frac{1}{2}+\frac{1}{2}=1$$

$$\frac{2}{6}=\frac{1}{3}$$

$$\frac{4}{3}=\frac{8}{6}$$

$$\frac{4}{3}=\frac{8}{6}=1\frac{2}{6}=1\frac{1}{3}$$

15. Each person will eat $\frac{4}{5}$ of a pancake, which is $\frac{1}{5}$ of the total pancakes.

16. One share will be $\frac{2}{4}$ or $\frac{1}{2}$ of a 6-pack. Each share is $\frac{1}{4}$ of the unit.

17. Student B used the least sophisticated strategy. The student split apart every 6-pack to make individual cans and then distributed them to the 3 children. Student C used the most sophisticated strategy because he or she use the least amount of cutting (separating) and marking. This student merely distributed entire 6-packs as far as possible, then distributed individual cans as necessary. Student A's strategy is between the other two in sophistication. Although student A distributed 6-packs, he or she needed to mark the individual components of the 6-packs. Notice how the student drew each individual can within the 6-pack. The need to mark individual components of a composite unit is usually a sign that a student is in a transitional stage: he or she is beginning to think in terms of composite units, but still needs some visual reassurance that each person is getting the same number of cans.

18. The strategies used by students A and B are very similar. Both marked every pizza so that it showed twice as many pieces as were needed for 3 people. Both used relatively unsophisticated strategies. However, when student A went to cut the fourth pizza, he or she noticed that each person would get two pieces of it and so it was not necessary to make as many cuts as were originally planned. In other words, the

student noticed that $\frac{2}{6} = \frac{1}{3}$ and cut the pizza more economically than it was marked. Student B gave each person $\frac{1}{6} + \frac{1}{6}$ of the fourth pizza. Thus, one share was more fragmented.

19. a. A more sophisticated strategy than either student used would be one in which pieces that were distributed as whole pieces were not marked:

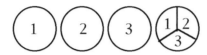

b. A strategy between the given two in sophistication might be

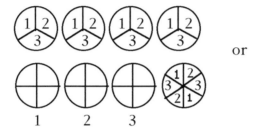

or

20. Figure out the number of cuts that it would take to accomplish each of the partitions. Student A's strategy requires 6 cuts; B's requires 4 cuts; C's requires 10 cuts; and D's requires 8 cuts. You can see that students A and B anticipated that a share would consist of 4 small rectangles, and they made some effort to keep each share connected. Students C and D were unable to anticipate that a share would consist of 4 rectangles, so they started by distributing 1 or 2 at a time. Ranking by sophistication (connectedness of shares), we get B, A, D, and C, from highest to lowest.

Chapter 7
Rational Numbers as Operators

1.   Operators which are improper fractions (fractions in which the numerator is larger than the denominator) will enlarge and proper fraction operators (those whose numerator is smaller than their denominator) will reduce.

2. The operator "$\frac{5}{3}$ of" enlarges a unit by a factor of 5 and reduces it by a factor of 3, so the ultimate result is enlargement.

3. Any operator whose denominator is larger than its numerator will do.

4. $\frac{3}{12}$ or $\frac{1}{4}$ because $\frac{1}{3} \cdot \frac{3}{4} = \frac{3}{12} = \frac{1}{4}$.

5.   If $\frac{5}{9}$ of the teachers are female, $\frac{4}{9}$ are male. If $\frac{3}{8}$ of the males are single, then $\frac{3}{8} \cdot \frac{4}{9}$ or $\frac{1}{6}$ are single males. If $\frac{1}{3}$ of the single males are over 50, $\frac{2}{3}$ are under 50. So $\frac{2}{3} \cdot \frac{1}{6} = \frac{1}{9}$ are single males under 50.

6. The starting quantity is multiplied by 3, then the result is divided by 6. In symbols, we could write $\frac{1}{6}(3 \cdot 8) = 4$. The composite operation is multiplication by $\frac{1}{2}$ and $\frac{1}{2}$ of 8 or $\frac{1}{2}(8) = 4$.

7. $\frac{2}{5}(\frac{3}{8}(1)) = \frac{6}{40}$

8.

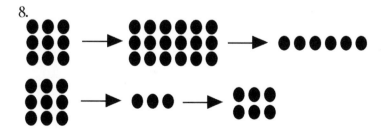

9. The first operator must be "$\frac{1}{2}$ of" (it exchanged 1 for 2) and the second, $\frac{1}{5}$ (an exchange of 1 for 5). $\frac{1}{2}$ must be larger because the second machine returned less than half.

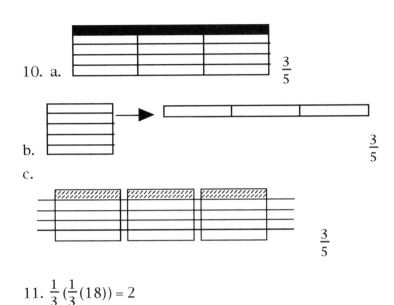

10. a. $\frac{3}{5}$

b. $\frac{3}{5}$

c.

                                                        $\frac{3}{5}$

11. $\frac{1}{3}(\frac{1}{3}(18)) = 2$

12. The results are equivalent.

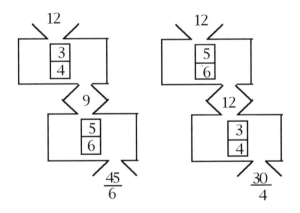

13. "$\frac{2}{9}$ of" means

a. take 2 copies of $\frac{1}{9}$ of a unit; or
b. take 1 of 9 equal shares of 1(2-unit); or
c. take 1 of 9 equal shares of 2(1-units)

14.

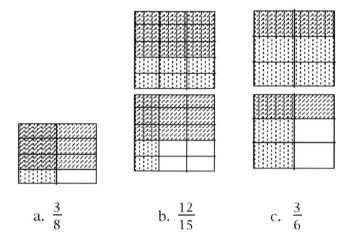

a. $\frac{3}{8}$ b. $\frac{12}{15}$ c. $\frac{3}{6}$

15.

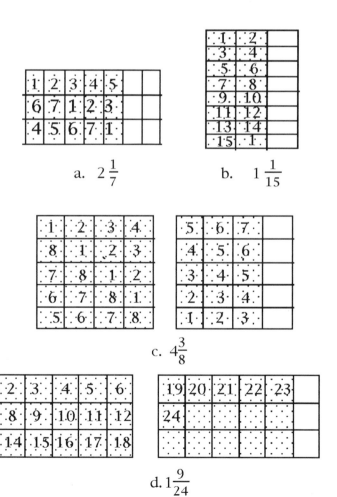

a. $2\frac{1}{7}$ b. $1\frac{1}{15}$

c. $4\frac{3}{8}$

d. $1\frac{9}{24}$

16. 16 children is $\frac{1}{3}$ the total number of people, so the total number of people is 48. The number of men is $\frac{3}{4}$ ($\frac{2}{3}$ (48)) = 24. The number of women is $\frac{1}{4}(\frac{2}{3}(48)) = 8$.

17. $\frac{5}{6} = \frac{15}{18}$ and $\frac{4}{9} = \frac{8}{18}$

18.

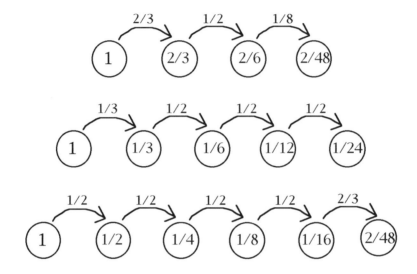

Chapter 8
Rational Numbers as Measures

1. 12 subintervals = $\frac{2}{3}$, so 6 subintervals = $\frac{1}{3}$, and 18 subintervals = 1 unit interval. Now we know that each subinterval is $\frac{1}{18}$ of the unit, so X, being 8 subintervals long, represents $\frac{8}{18}$.

2. 3 subintervals = $\frac{1}{5}$, so 1 unit interval = 15 subintervals. X = $\frac{13}{15}$.

3. 18 subintervals = $\frac{9}{4}$, so $\frac{1}{4}$ = 2 subintervals and 1 unit interval = 8 subintervals. X = $\frac{3}{8}$.

4. 10 subintervals = $\frac{5}{6}$, so 2 subintervals = $\frac{1}{6}$ and 1 unit interval = 12 subintervals. X = $\frac{3}{12}$.

5. 12 subintervals = $\frac{3}{4}$, so 4 subintervals = $\frac{1}{4}$ and 1 unit interval = 16 subintervals. X = $\frac{7}{16}$.

6. 6 subintervals = $\frac{1}{3}$, so 1 unit interval = 18 subintervals. X= $\frac{8}{18}$.

7. 8 subintervals = $\frac{4}{3}$; 2 subintervals = $\frac{1}{3}$; and 1 subinterval = $\frac{1}{6}$. So $\frac{5}{6}$ must be 5 subintervals long.

8. 2 subintervals = $\frac{1}{4}$, so 1 must be $\frac{1}{8}$, and 7 must be $\frac{7}{8}$.

9. If 4 subintervals $= \frac{1}{3}$, then 12 must be 1 unit interval. Partition each of the 12 into 2 equal pieces to get twenty-fourths. Then 7 subunits gives $\frac{7}{24}$.

$$0 \qquad \qquad \frac{7}{24} \; \frac{1}{3} \qquad \qquad \qquad \qquad 1$$

10. 3 subunits $= \frac{1}{6}$, so 18 subunits = 1 unit interval. Partition each interval in the unit into 4 equal pieces to get seventy-seconds. Then $\frac{3}{8}$ will consist of 27 of those subintervals or $\frac{27}{72}$.

11. a. By successively partitioning, you can see that you have about $\frac{23}{32}$ of a tank. Answers may vary due to accuracy in partitioning, but you should get a result close to .71.

b. $\frac{7}{16}$ tank or close to .44

12. a. You have $\frac{10}{16}$ or $\frac{5}{8}$ of a gallon left.

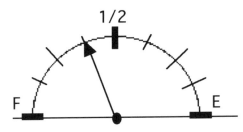

b. You were able to buy about 3.5 gallons. (4.00 ÷ $1.139 = 3.512). Because the tank holds 14 gallons, that is $\frac{1}{4}$ tank ($\frac{3.5}{14}$).

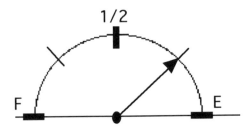

c. By successively partitioning, you can see that you have about $\frac{3}{32}$ of a tank left. (Again, due to the inaccuracy of partitioning, you may get a slightly different result, but it should be in the ball park of .09.) This means that you used $\frac{29}{32}$ of a tank, which was about 11 gallons of gas (340 ÷ 31 = 10.967). So if you divide the 11 gallons divided into 29 parts, then you would have $\frac{1}{32}$ of a tank, and 32 times that amount would be a full tank. $\frac{11}{29}(32) = 12.14$ gallons.

13. Picture the candles next to each other, and note their burning time in hours and the fraction of each candle remaining after each hour. By successive partitioning, first to eighteenths and then to thirty-sixths, you will see that between 4 hours and 5 hours of burning time, candle A (the longer-burning candle) is twice as long as B (the shorter-burning candle). At exactly $4\frac{1}{2}$ hours, candle A has $\frac{18}{36}$ of it height remaining and candle B has $\frac{9}{36}$ of its height remaining.

14. Please remember that there is more than one correct way to write these fractions as the sum of unit fraction. Only one method is given here.
a. Think about the way in which you might partition a unit interval containing this fraction. If you partitioned it into sixths, then $\frac{2}{3}$ would be $\frac{4}{6}$ from which you can measure out $\frac{1}{2}$ and then $\frac{1}{6}$.
b. When the unit interval containing $\frac{3}{5}$ is partitioned into tenths, $\frac{3}{5}$ becomes $\frac{6}{10}$, from which you can measure out $\frac{1}{2}$, then $\frac{1}{10}$.
c. $\frac{5}{6} = \frac{1}{2} + \frac{1}{3}$
d. $\frac{7}{9} = \frac{1}{2} + \frac{1}{6} + \frac{1}{9}$
e. $\frac{13}{14} = \frac{1}{2} + \frac{1}{4} + \frac{1}{7} + \frac{1}{28}$
f. $\frac{23}{24} = \frac{1}{2} + \frac{1}{4} + \frac{1}{8} + \frac{1}{12}$

15. a. By successive partitioning of the view strip, you get $\frac{25}{32}$ (or something close to .78) of a bottle remaining. This is 25 ounces.

Problem 13

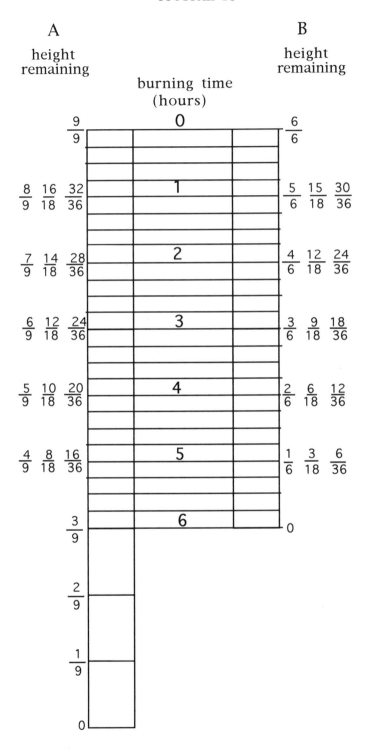

b. By successive partitioning, you get $\frac{3}{16}$ (or something close to .19) of a bottle remaining. This is 6 ounces.

c. By successive partitioning, you get $\frac{21}{32}$ (or something close to .66) bottle or 21 ounces.

16. By successively partitioning 1 hour, obtain twelfths. This produces 6 subintervals in the half hour. The arrow should point to $\frac{5}{12}$ since 25 minutes is $\frac{5}{12}$ of 1 hour. (Your answer may be close.)

17. (Your answer may be close.)

a. By successive partitioning, obtaining $\frac{54}{64}$ and $\frac{57}{64}$ for the given points. Then $\frac{55}{64}$ and $\frac{56}{64}$ lie between them.

b. By successive partitioning, obtain $\frac{11}{32}$ and $\frac{14}{32}$ for the given points. Then $\frac{12}{32}$ and $\frac{13}{32}$ lie between them.

18. When you measure the point's distance with your metric ruler, you should get .21. On your first three trials, if you were fairly accurate in your partitioning, you should have ended up with fraction equivalents of the decimal .21—or something close to it. For example, if you ended up with $\frac{13}{60}$, your decimal equivalent would be .2166. Or if you ended up with $\frac{7}{32}$, your decimal equivalent would be .21875. That's pretty close, especially because you were just eye-balling the partitions, not measuring them! If your first two decimal places were not .21, then you may want to try it again.

19. a. On a number line, choose a unit interval, and then partition it until you have points corresponding to each of the numbers . When you have partitioned the unit interval into twenty-fourths, you will see that
$\frac{5}{6} < \frac{21}{24} < \frac{11}{12}$.
b. When your unit interval is partitioned into eighteenths, you will see that $\frac{3}{9} < \frac{1}{2} < \frac{15}{18}$.

c. When your unit interval is partitioned into twenty-eighths, you will see that $\frac{6}{7} < \frac{13}{14} < \frac{27}{28}$. Note that these numbers are $1 - \frac{1}{7}$, $1 - \frac{1}{14}$, $1 - \frac{1}{28}$.

20. a. By partitioning a unit interval until you have thirtieths, you can rename $\frac{1}{6}$ as $\frac{5}{30}$ and $\frac{1}{5}$ as $\frac{6}{30}$. If you next cut each subinterval in half, thus creating sixtieths, you will get only one fraction name between the given fractions. So next, partition each subinterval into thirds, thus creating ninetieths. Then your given fractions are $\frac{15}{90}$ and $\frac{18}{90}$. $\frac{16}{90}$ and $\frac{17}{90}$ both lie between them.

b. We can partition the interval between $\frac{9}{10}$ and $\frac{10}{10}$ into 3 equal subintervals and then each would be renamed as $\frac{27}{30}$ and $\frac{30}{30}$, with $\frac{28}{30}$ and $\frac{29}{30}$ lying between them.

21. Each of the boys has $\frac{1}{3}$ of the big licorice stick. Imagine that they could put their pieces back together and partition the licorice stick into twelfths. Then each boy's share is $\frac{1}{3}$ or $\frac{4}{12}$. If they had originally split the candy 4 ways, each would get $\frac{3}{12}$. This means that if each boy cuts off $\frac{1}{4}$ of his share for the newcomer, every boy will have $\frac{3}{12}$ or $\frac{1}{4}$ of the candy.

22. Write $\frac{1}{5}$ as sixths: $\frac{1}{5} = \frac{1\frac{1}{5}}{6}$. Now find fractions between $\frac{1}{6}$ and $\frac{1\frac{1}{5}}{6}$ by choosing as many fractions as you need that are less than $\frac{1\frac{1}{5}}{6}$: $\frac{1\frac{1}{6}}{6}$, $\frac{1\frac{1}{7}}{6}$, $\frac{1\frac{1}{8}}{6}$, etc. Then $\frac{1\frac{1}{5}}{6} = \frac{6}{30}$, $\frac{1\frac{1}{7}}{6} = \frac{\frac{8}{7}}{6} = \frac{8}{42}$, and $\frac{1\frac{1}{8}}{6} = \frac{\frac{9}{8}}{6} = \frac{9}{48}$.

Chapter 9
Quantitative Relationships:
Visual and Verbal

1. The task of drawing a knife, fork, and spoon turns out to be a very difficult task because you have to keep track of several sets of proportions at the same time: the size of teach utensil's handle as compared to the top part of it, the size of the utensils in relation to each other, and the size of the utensils in relation to the plate. Students are not always able to coordinate all of these relations.

2. To draw the woman next to the car, you must visualize yourself standing next to a car and figure out approximately what part of your height the height of the car would be. The car is about $\frac{15}{16}$" high in the picture. If you imagine that the height of the car is close to $\frac{3}{4}$ the height of an adult, then, in order to draw her in proportion to the size of her car, we should make Mrs. Jones about $1\frac{1}{4}$ inches tall.

3. In a caricature, the artist deliberately draws some feature(s) out of proportion to the rest of the face or body. Sometimes, the intention may be to emphasize a particular characteristic of the person. For example, the first caricature is one of Mark Twain, and the artist may have been trying to capture something of his character. His long, white hair and mustache give him a kindly, grandfatherly appearance. His ear is way out of proportion with the rest of his head, perhaps suggesting that he would be a good listener, like a grandfather to whom you could go when you had a problem. Sometimes the artist is trying to reflect personal or popular sentiment about a person. This is usually the case in the caricature of a political figure. In the second picture, the artist depicts Prince Charles with a head out of proportion to the rest of his body. Charles' ears, which normally stand out from his head, are drawn out of proportion to the rest of his head, thus giving him a "Dumbo" look. This caricature gives a double message. The artist sees Charles as a person who thinks highly of himself, and at the same time is rather stupid-looking in the eyes of the public.

4. The pizza was not distributed fairly among the three groups. The 45 students received a smaller portion of the pizza than the 45 parents and teachers received and the parents received a larger portion than the teachers.

5.   You will be surprised at how many students do not understand stretching and shrinking. A common misconception is that if an object becomes smaller or shorter along one dimension, it has shrunk. Many younger students will think that the cat has shrunk because he is shorter. They focus on height and fail to notice that the heads and tails and feet are the same size. It is important to help students realize that shrinking means that all of the dimensions of an object change. It is easy enough to help them think about why the shorter cat is not the shrunken version of the larger cat. "Look at the length of you arm right now. If you were shrunk to a height of 2 feet, would your arms be the same length they are right now?"

6.   For most children through sixth or seventh grade, this question is very difficult. Their reasoning becomes confused because they introduce the idea that the larger wheel takes longer to make one full turn. Turning faster and going farther enter into their discussion and they lose sight of the fact that the wheels are both attached to the same tractor and must move forward or backward at the same rate.   Even when they get that idea straightened out, the favorite response is that the front wheel has to go farther in order for the back wheel to get off the field. Visualizing the task usually proves to be too much and a demonstrations is needed. Start measuring the distance each wheel covers as soon as the first wheel enter the field and stop measuring when the back wheel leaves the field. Students need to be convinced that both wheels cover the same distance. Then they can explore another relevant question: Do both wheels make the same number of turns to cross the field? The answer is no. The smaller wheel will have turned a larger number of times to cover the same distance as the larger wheel.

7. As always, answers are not necessarily unique.

picture:frame :: yard:fence   R : is enclosed by

giraffe:neck :: porcupine:quills   R : is best known for

food:body :: rain:earth   R : nourishes

car:gasoline :: sail:wind   R : is fueled by

sap:tree :: blood:body   R : flows through

sandwich:boy :: carrot:rabbit   R : is food for

pear:tree :: potato:ground   R : is grown in

tree:leaves :: book:pages   R : is composed of

conductor:train :: captain:ship   R : is the commander of

wedding:bride :: funeral:corpse   R : is a ceremony for

8. a. To decorate the larger cookie so that the mixture looks the same as the mixture on the smaller cookie, both the density and the relative numbers of sprinkles and chocolate chips should be the same.

b. The area of the larger cookies is actually about 4 times that of the smaller cookie, and so there should be 4 times as many sprinkles and chocolate chips. Check yourself. The smaller cookie had the same number of pieces of each topping, so your large cookie should have 28 sprinkles and 28 chocolate chips.

9. a. 5 pieces in half the candy bar

b. 2 pieces in $\frac{1}{5}$ the candy bar

c. 7 pieces in $\frac{1}{2} + \frac{1}{5}$

d. $\frac{7}{10}$ of the candy bar

e. $\frac{3}{10}$ of the candy bar

f. $\frac{1}{2} - \frac{1}{5} = \frac{3}{10}$

g. 1 piece

h. $\frac{1}{5}$ of $\frac{1}{2}$ is $\frac{1}{10}$

i. $2\frac{1}{2}$ times

j. $\frac{1}{2} \div \frac{1}{5} = 2\frac{1}{2}$

10.
a. 1 to 2
b. 1 to 3
c. 1 to 3
d. 1 to 1

11. Of course, the answer depends on the height of the person answering the question. Assume that the height of the dog is roughly $\frac{1}{4}$ the height of the person (using knee, waist, chest, top of head as

quarter marks). Also assume that the person answering is about 5 feet tall. That means the dog would be about $1\frac{1}{4}$ feet high. Then if we increase proportionately, the person grows to $1\frac{3}{5}$ of his or her height, or just under $1\frac{1}{2}$ times his or her height. The dog must do the same. This would make the dog just under 2 feet or about $1\frac{7}{8}$ feet high.

12. a. Red is half of purple, but purple is not half of dark green. Another way to look at it: Purple covers $\frac{2}{3}$ of dark green, but red covers only half of the purple. Replace purple with light green.

b. White is $\frac{1}{5}$ the length of yellow, but light green is $\frac{3}{10}$ the length of orange. Another way to look at it: Orange is twice as long as yellow, but light green is not twice as long as white. Replace light green with red.

c. White is $\frac{1}{3}$ of light green, but light green is half of dark green. Another way to look at it: light green is 3 times as long as white, but dark green is not three times as long as light green. Replace the dark green with blue.

13.

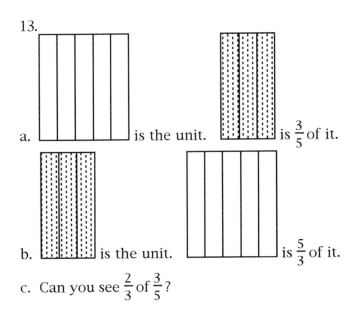

a. ⬜ is the unit. ⬜ is $\frac{3}{5}$ of it.

b. ⬜ is the unit. ⬜ is $\frac{5}{3}$ of it.

c. Can you see $\frac{2}{3}$ of $\frac{3}{5}$?

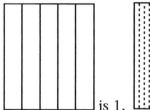 is 1. is $\frac{3}{5}$ of it.

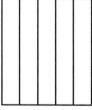 is $\frac{2}{3}$ of ($\frac{3}{5}$ of 1) or $\frac{2}{5}$ of 1.

d. Can you see $\frac{5}{3}$ of $\frac{3}{5}$?

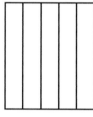 is the unit.  is $\frac{3}{5}$ of it.

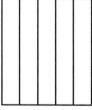 in relation to 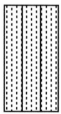 is $\frac{5}{3}$ of ($\frac{3}{5}$ of 1).

e. 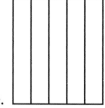 is the unit. 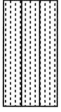 is $\frac{3}{5}$ of it.

How many ($\frac{3}{5}$ of 1) are in 1? $1\frac{2}{3}$.

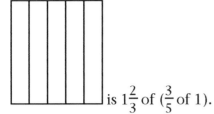 is $1\frac{2}{3}$ of ($\frac{3}{5}$ of 1).

f.  is the unit. 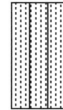 is $\frac{3}{5}$ of it.

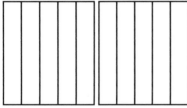 is 2. How many 2s are in $\frac{3}{5}$? $\frac{3}{5}$ is $\frac{3}{10}$ of 2. So

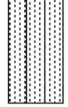 is $\frac{3}{5}$ of 1 = $\frac{3}{10}$ of 2.

g. If 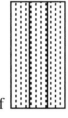 is $\frac{3}{4}$ of 1, then  is 1 and  is $\frac{5}{4}$. How many ($\frac{3}{4}$ of 1) are in ($\frac{5}{4}$ of 1)? $1\frac{2}{3}$.

So 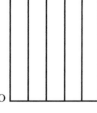 is $1\frac{2}{3}$ units of ($\frac{3}{4}$ of 1).

14. a. Dianne was faster today.
b. She was slower today.
c. She was faster today.
d. She was faster today.
e. We could not draw any conclusions if Dianne ran fewer laps in less time than she did yesterday, or if she ran more laps in more time than she did yesterday.

15. You may have other questions. Here are some possibilities.

Addition. If you used $\frac{1}{3}$ of the eggs, how many did you use? If I used $\frac{1}{4}$ of the eggs, how many did I use? How many of the eggs did we use? What part of the carton did we use? $\frac{1}{3} + \frac{1}{4} = \frac{7}{12}$

Subtraction. Who used more? How much more? $\frac{1}{3} - \frac{1}{4} = \frac{1}{12}$

Multiplication. How much is a half of a third of the carton? $\frac{1}{2} \cdot \frac{1}{3} = \frac{2}{12}$.

Division. How many times will $\frac{1}{4}$ fit into $\frac{1}{3}$? $\frac{1}{3} \div \frac{1}{4} = 1\frac{1}{3}$

Chapter 10
Reasoning With Fractions

1. Fifths are shown using horizontal divisions and sixths are shown using vertical divisions. Essentially, this double partitioning process produces a common denominator. When $\frac{4}{5}$ is shaded, $\frac{24}{30}$ of the unit is shaded, and when $\frac{5}{6}$ is shaded, $\frac{25}{30}$ of the unit is shaded. Thus, $\frac{5}{6}$ is greater.

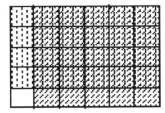

2. a. CRP $\frac{8}{14}$ is greater than $\frac{1}{2}$ and $\frac{4}{9}$ is less than $\frac{1}{2}$. So $\frac{8}{14} > \frac{4}{9}$.

b. SNP $\frac{3}{17}$ and $\frac{3}{19}$ each have the same number of pieces, and so the critical question becomes "What size are the pieces?" Seventeenths are larger than nineteenths, so $\frac{3}{17} > \frac{3}{19}$.

c. SSP   Because both fractions involve thirteenths, the decision about which is larger can be made by asking how many of those identical pieces each fraction contains. $\frac{5}{13} < \frac{8}{13}$.

d. SNP $\frac{3}{2} = 1\frac{1}{2}$, while $\frac{4}{3} = 1\frac{1}{3}$. Both mixed numbers are between 1 unit and 2 units and we need only compare their fractional parts. Because numerators are the same, we need to compare the size of the pieces. Because $\frac{1}{2} > \frac{1}{3}$, $1\frac{1}{2} > 1\frac{1}{3}$ and $\frac{3}{2} > \frac{4}{3}$.

3. a. $\frac{7}{13} = \frac{7\frac{7}{13}}{14}$, so to find fractions between $\frac{7}{14}$ and $\frac{7\frac{7}{13}}{14}$ choose numerators greater than 7 and less than $7\frac{7}{13}$. For example, choose $7\frac{6}{13}$, $7\frac{5}{13}$, and $7\frac{4}{13}$. Then $\frac{7\frac{6}{13}}{14} = \frac{97}{102}$ and $\frac{7\frac{5}{13}}{14} = \frac{96}{102}$ and $\frac{7\frac{4}{13}}{14} = \frac{95}{102}$ between the given fractions.

b. To obtain fractions between $\frac{6}{8}$ and $\frac{7}{8}$, choose numerators between 6 and 7, say $6\frac{1}{3}$, $6\frac{1}{4}$, and $6\frac{1}{5}$. Then $\frac{6\frac{1}{3}}{8} = \frac{19}{24}$, $\frac{6\frac{1}{4}}{8} = \frac{25}{32}$, and $\frac{6\frac{1}{5}}{8} = \frac{31}{40}$ are between the given fractions.

4. a. more adults
b. number of adults = twice the number of children
c. number of children = $\frac{1}{2}$ number of adults

5 a. To construct the smallest possible sum, you will need the larger numbers in the denominators, so make one denominator 7 and the other 8. Then put the 6 with the 8 so that you get a larger number of smaller pieces.

$$\frac{5}{7} + \frac{6}{8}$$

b. To construct the largest possible sum, you will need pieces of larger size, so use 5 and the 6 as denominators. Make 8 the numerator for the 5 so that you get a larger number of larger pieces.

$$\frac{8}{5} + \frac{7}{6}$$

c. To construct the smallest positive difference, you want to make the fractions as close as possible in size and you want the largest numbers in the denominator so that the difference is very small. Fifty-sixths will be smaller than thirtieths, forty-seconds, or fortieths.

$$\frac{6}{8} - \frac{5}{7}$$

d. To construct the largest difference, first create the largest fraction, and then, with the remaining numbers, the smallest fraction.

$$\frac{8}{5} - \frac{6}{7}$$

e. To construct the smallest possible product, choose the denominators to give the smallest- size pieces. After you choose 8 and 7 as denominators, it does not matter which numerator is 5 and which is 6.

$$\frac{5}{8} \times \frac{6}{7} \quad \text{or} \quad \frac{6}{8} \times \frac{5}{7}$$

f. To construct the largest possible product, you want the largest possible numerators, so choose 8 and 7. Then 5 and 6 may be placed in either of the denominators.

$$\frac{8}{6} \times \frac{7}{5} \quad \text{or} \quad \frac{8}{5} \times \frac{7}{6}$$

g. To construct the smallest quotient, the divisor should be as large as possible, so choose $\frac{8}{5}$ as the divisor. Then the dividend should be as small as possible.

$$\frac{6}{7} \div \frac{8}{5}$$

h. To construct the largest quotient, the dividend should be as large as possible, so choose $\frac{8}{5}$. The divisor should be as small as possible.

$$\frac{8}{5} \div \frac{6}{7}$$

6. We observe that the large bucket and 3 small buckets hold the same amount as 1 medium bucket and 5 small buckets. 4 medium buckets hold the same amount as 5 small buckets. Therefore, the large bucket and 3 small buckets hold more—in fact, 1 medium bucket more—than 4 medium buckets.

7. 1 medium bucket must hold $7\frac{3}{8}$ liters, so 1 small bucket must hold $2\frac{1}{3}$ liters less, or $5\frac{1}{24}$ liters.

8. Because a medium and three small buckets hold 11 liters, 11 liters and 1 large bucketful are $16\frac{2}{3}$ liters. This means that 1 large bucket hold $5\frac{2}{3}$ liters. Then 2 small buckets must hold $4\frac{1}{3}$ liters and 1 small holds $2\frac{1}{6}$ liters. Three small buckets hold $6\frac{1}{2}$ liters and 1 medium holds $4\frac{1}{2}$ liters.

9. Comparing the two quantities, we see that 1 medium bucket must hold the same amount as 2 small buckets. This would mean that 5 small buckets hold 12 liters; 1 small bucket holds $2\frac{2}{5}$ liters. 1 medium bucket must then hold $4\frac{4}{5}$ liters.

10.   a. There are more students because they are $\frac{5}{8}$ of the town, while others comprise $\frac{3}{8}$ of the town.

b. $\frac{5}{8}$ (the number of students) is 1 times the number of nonstudents ($\frac{3}{8}$)

plus another $\frac{2}{8}$. The $\frac{2}{8}$ is 2 out of the 3 parts in $\frac{3}{8}$. Therefore, the number

of students is $1\frac{2}{3}$ times the number of nonstudents.

c. Nonstudents ($\frac{3}{8}$) is 3 out of the 5 parts in $\frac{5}{8}$. So the number of

nonstudents is $\frac{3}{5}$ of the number of students.

11. a. The fraction gets larger.
b. You can not tell.
c. The fraction gets smaller.
d. You produce equivalent fractions. They have the same relative size.
e. The fraction gets smaller.

12. a. Mrs. Brown has more students.
b. Multiply by $\frac{5}{3}$.
c. Multiply by $\frac{3}{5}$.
d. Mrs. Brown has 45 students.
e. Mrs. Henderson has 18 students.

13. Many answers are possible. Here are some examples.
a. $\frac{99}{100}$ is very close to 1 = $\frac{100}{100}$. $\frac{99}{100} = \frac{297}{300}$ and 1 = $\frac{300}{300}$. So $\frac{298}{300}$ and $\frac{299}{300}$ are
even closer.

14. a. equivalence
b. $\frac{3}{5}$

c.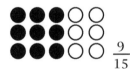

d. A fraction will be a clone of $\frac{3}{5}$ if you can rearrange the chips so that

you have copies of ●●●○○.

(i.) is not a clone because you get

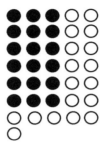

(ii.) is not a clone either, because you get

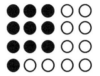

(iii.) is a clone because the chips can be rearranged to get

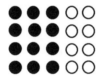

15. Jimmy made clones of $\frac{4}{6}$ and of $\frac{7}{9}$ until both clones had the same number of chips. When both had 18 chips, he could see that $\frac{14}{18}$, the clone of $\frac{7}{9}$, was greater than $\frac{12}{18}$, the clone of $\frac{4}{6}$.

16. a. Make clones of $\frac{5}{6}$.

$\begin{array}{l}\text{●●●●●○}\\\text{●●●●●○}\end{array} = \frac{10}{12}$ $\begin{array}{l}\text{●●●●●○}\\\text{●●●●●○}\\\text{●●●●●○}\end{array} = \frac{15}{18}$

The 3-copy clone has 18 chips, so it may be compared to $\frac{13}{18}$.

$\frac{5}{6} > \frac{13}{18}$ because $\frac{15}{18} > \frac{13}{18}$.

b. Make clones of both fractions until you get the same number of chips in both clones.

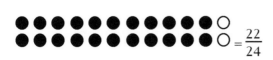 $= \frac{22}{24}$ 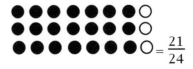 $= \frac{21}{24}$

$\frac{11}{12} > \frac{7}{8}$ because $\frac{22}{24} > \frac{21}{24}$.

c. 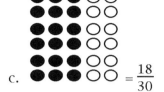 $= \frac{18}{30}$ 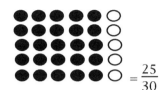 $= \frac{25}{30}$

$\frac{3}{5} < \frac{5}{6}$ because $\frac{18}{30} < \frac{25}{30}$.

17. $\frac{9}{10}$ of a pound will cost less than 1 pounds costs. If 1 pound costs $3.85, then $\frac{1}{10}$ of a pound costs $.385 . So $\frac{9}{10}$ of a pound costs $.38\frac{1}{2}$ less than the cost of 1 pound or $3.47.

18. a. $\frac{3}{7} < \frac{5}{8}$ because $\frac{3}{7}$ is less than $\frac{1}{2}$ and $\frac{5}{8}$ is greater than $\frac{1}{2}$.

b. $3\frac{1}{2}$ is half of 7 and $2\frac{1}{2}$ is half of 5. So $\frac{3}{7}$ is $\frac{\frac{1}{2}}{7}$ less than $\frac{1}{2}$ and $\frac{5}{8}$ is $\frac{\frac{1}{2}}{5}$ less than $\frac{1}{2}$. $\frac{\frac{1}{2}}{7}$ is smaller than $\frac{\frac{1}{2}}{5}$, so $\frac{3}{7} > \frac{2}{5}$.

c. $\frac{4}{9}$ is $\frac{\frac{1}{2}}{9}$ less than $\frac{1}{2}$ and $\frac{5}{11}$ is $\frac{\frac{1}{2}}{11}$ less than $\frac{1}{2}$. Because $\frac{\frac{1}{2}}{11} < \frac{\frac{1}{2}}{9}$, $\frac{5}{11}$ is closer to $\frac{1}{2}$. $\frac{5}{11} > \frac{4}{9}$.

d. $\frac{5}{9} > \frac{2}{5}$ because $\frac{2}{5} < \frac{1}{2}$ and $\frac{5}{9} > \frac{1}{2}$.

e. $\frac{3}{8} < \frac{5}{9}$ because $\frac{3}{8} < \frac{1}{2}$ and $\frac{5}{9} > \frac{1}{2}$.

f. $\frac{3}{7}$ is $\frac{\frac{1}{2}}{7}$ or $\frac{1}{14}$ less than $\frac{1}{2}$, and $\frac{5}{12}$ is $\frac{1}{12}$ less than $\frac{1}{2}$. So $\frac{3}{7}$ is closer to $\frac{1}{2}$ and $\frac{3}{7} > \frac{5}{12}$.

g. $\frac{7}{12} > \frac{6}{11}$ because $\frac{6}{11}$ is $\frac{\frac{1}{2}}{11} = \frac{1}{22}$ more than $\frac{1}{2}$ and $\frac{7}{12}$ is $\frac{1}{12}$ more than $\frac{1}{2}$.

19. We want to find the fraction of the man's daily supply that the woman is now drinking. If his 24-day supply is now supplying two of them for 18 days, then we might picture it like this:

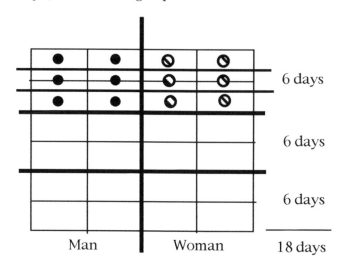

The water that the man used in 8 days is now being used by the two of them in 6 days. Half of that is being used by the woman, so she is drinking 4 day's worth of the man's water in 6 days, and 2 days' worth in 3 days, and $\frac{2}{3}$ one of his daily rations in 1 day.

20. The boys have 1 pizza for 3 boys. If you give 1 pizza to each group of 3 girls, then there is 1 pizza for the last girl. After she takes the same amount as the other girls had (quotient: $\frac{1}{3}$ pizza), then there is $\frac{2}{3}$ pizza extra. The girls have more pizza than the boys.

21. An upper bound on the number of scouts who could have all four items is 70%. Because only 70% had a compass, it would be impossible to find a larger number of people who had all four items. What is the smallest number? If 85% have a watch, then 15% do not. When we look for the 85% who also have a knife, the largest number without watches may be included in the 85%. So only 70% may have both. When we look for the 75% with matches, we may get the largest number of people who did not have all of the previous items, 30%. Thus, we have only 45% who definitely have all three items. Similarly, when we choose the 70% who have a compass, we may include the largest percent who did not have the previous items, 55%. Thus, only 15% definitely have all four items.

22. a. $1\frac{1}{2} \times \frac{1}{4} = \frac{1}{4} + \frac{1}{8} = \frac{3}{8}$

b. $2\frac{1}{4} \times 4 = 8 + 1 = 9$

c. $3 \times 2\frac{1}{8} = 6 + \frac{3}{8} = 6\frac{3}{8}$

d. $2\frac{2}{3} \times 6\frac{1}{2} = 12 + 1\,(13) + 4\,(17) + \frac{1}{3} = 17\frac{1}{3}$

e. $1\frac{1}{5} \times 2\frac{1}{2} = 2 + \frac{1}{2}\,(2\frac{1}{2}) + \frac{2}{5}\,(2\frac{9}{10}) + \frac{1}{10} = 3$

f. $2\frac{1}{3} \times 4\frac{1}{2} = 8 + 1\,(9) + 1\frac{1}{3}\,(10\frac{1}{3}) + \frac{1}{6} = 10\frac{1}{2}$

Chapter 11
Ratios

1. a. 2 boys:3 girls

b. The number of cows is $\frac{4}{5}$ the number of pigs, so the ratio of cows to pigs is 4:5.

c. The ratio of Mary's height to her mom's height is 2:3.

d. The ratio of Dan's weight to Becky's weight is 5:2.

2. a. $\frac{2}{7}$

b. 2:5

3. a. $\frac{80}{100}$

b. 30 balcony:70 floor

c. 20 empty:80 occupied seats

d. 2 empty:1 occupied in the balcony

4. a. The small gear makes $1\frac{3}{8}$ turns every time the large gear turns around once.

b. When the small gear has made 5 turns, the large gear has made $3\frac{7}{11}$ turns.

c. 4 turns of the small gear uses 32 teeth, so the large gear would need $32 \div \frac{4}{3}$ or 24 teeth.

d. 4 turns of the large gear would require 44 teeth, so the small gear would need $44 \div \frac{11}{3} = 12$ teeth.

5. a. 3:4 is greater than 5:9 or you have a better chance of winning with the odds 3:4 than with the odds 5:9.

b. The picture shows that 3:4 = 15:20 and 5:9 = 15:27.   This means that both ratios show 15 fors, but 5:9 has 7 more againsts.

c. 3(5:9) - 5(3:4) = (0: 7)

6. Other pictures are possible, depending on which fraction or ratio you clone.

a. 11:12 is greater because, after removing copies of 5:6, we have 1:0.

11:12- 2(5:6) = 1:0

b. 12:16 and 3:4 are equivalent because cloning one produces the other.
4(3:4)=12:16

c. Cloning 5:8 and removing 5 copies of 7:9, we see that we get 0 for: 11 against, so 5:8 is less than 7:9. 7(5:8) - 5(7:9) = 0:11

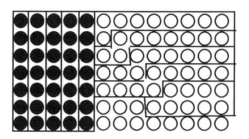

d. Make 5 copies of $\frac{7}{8}$ and 4 copies of $\frac{9}{10}$. The clone of $\frac{7}{8}$ is $\frac{35}{40}$.
Rearranging the clone of $\frac{9}{10}$, we can see that it is $\frac{36}{40}$. Therefore, $\frac{9}{10} > \frac{7}{8}$.

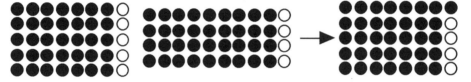

e. Make 9 copies of 7:8 and remove 7 copies of 9:10 to get 0:2.

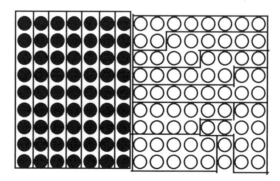

f. Clone $\frac{4}{9}$ and $\frac{3}{10}$ until there are 90 in each set. Rearrange the $\frac{4}{9}$ clone
to get $\frac{40}{90}$ and compare to the $\frac{3}{10}$ clone, which is $\frac{27}{90}$. $\frac{4}{9} > \frac{3}{10}$.

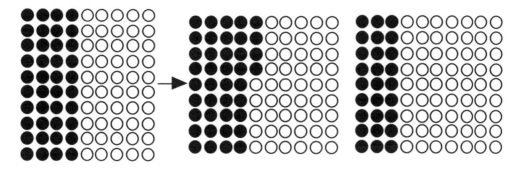

g. Removing copies of 4:5 from 8:15, we get 0:5. Therefore, 4:5 is larger. 8:15 - 2(4:5) = 0:5.

7. Jennifer did not compare fractions; she compared ratios. She first cloned 3:4 and removed one copy of 5:8 to get 1:0. Then she cloned 5:8 and removed 5 copied of 3:4 to get 0:4. Her system for interpreting the results was unique. She interpreted the black dots as money (say, dollars) needed to gain entrance to a movie or a theater, or a show of some sort. The empty circles she interpreted as people who needed to get into the show. The price of $3 for 4 people or $6 for 8 people, is higher than the price of $5 for 8 people. Similarly, the price $5 for 8 people or $15 for 24 people is less than $15 for 20 people at the 3:4 rate.

8. a.

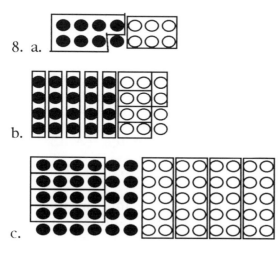

b.

c.

9. a. The ratio 3:6 is extendible over the people who are in the theater. Because the information about how many adults and how many children is already lost, we can further reduce this ratio, say, to 1:3.

b. The ratio is not extendible, and not reducible without loss of information. We cannot add to or subtract teeth from a gear. The ratio of teeth on the small gear to the number on the large gear is 30:45. Writing the ratio as 2:3 gives up size of the gear.

c. The ratio 12:14 is not extendible. We cannot add children to the classroom or increase the number of existing pets. In reducing the ratio, we lose the information about how many children are in the class.

d. The ratio is not extendible. For example, if the perimeter is 24, the area is 36, not 18. The ratio is also not reducible without losing information.

e. The ratio is extendible within the same bag of candies and to the extent that we don't go over the total number of pieces in the bag. The ratio is also reducible. For example, 3:6 = 1:2. Information about the number of candies has already been lost.

f. The ratio is not extendible. It will not be true again that the ratio of the child's age to the mother's age will be 4:6. The ratio is reducible to 2:3 without loss of information, because 4:6 does not give us present ages.

g. The ratio is not extendible. Dave will not be growing! If the ratio is reduced, we lose the information about both people's current heights.

h. The ratio $2.6: 4 oz. is extendible. We may assume that you can purchase more than 4 ounces at the same rate. The ratio is reducible to $.65 per 1 ounce.

i. The ratio is not extendible. The family has only 6 children. If the ratio is reduced, we lose the information about how many children are in the family.

10. a. .75 parking spaces per faculty member conveys the information that, on the average, less than one parking space per faculty member is needed.
b. 1.55 children per family is an average conveying the information that there are not enough children in the town to match 2 with each family.
c. Dividing this ratio would not serve any purpose. The ratio is applicable in only one situation.
d. .375 condos per family is an average conveying the information that the management company can work with 2 or almost 3 families for each condo it manages.
e. .4 computer per student is an average signifying that the school has almost enough computers to match 2 students with each computer.

11. The ratios are realistically only approximations, but if we assume that they are exact and that the number of students is not changing,

then the number of students has to be divisible by both 30 and 25 because we cannot hire fractions of teachers. $30 = 2 \cdot 3 \cdot 5$ and $25 = 5 \cdot 5$. So look at multiples of 150. If the school has 300 students, then it has 10 teachers, and $300:12 = 25:1$, so they would need to hire 2 more teachers. If the school has 450 students and 15 teachers, the $450:18$ gives the required ratio and they would need to hire 3 more teachers. Similarly, if the school has 600 students and 20 teachers, $600: 24 = 25:1$, so they would need to hire 4 more teachers. The number of teachers needed is 1 for every 150 students. This would be an approximate solution even if the given ratios were approximates.

12.

a.

		÷2	÷4	x5	
earth wt. (pounds)	160	80	20	100	120
Jupiter wt. (pounds)	416	208	52	260	260 + 52 = 312

b.

		x5	x2		
pizza	$\frac{3}{5}$	3	6	$\frac{12}{5}$	$6 + \frac{12}{5} = 8\frac{2}{5}$
people	1	5	10	4	14

x4

c.

		x3		x3	
dorm or home	3	9	$\frac{3}{4}$	$\frac{9}{4}$	$9 + \frac{9}{4} = 11\frac{1}{4}$ or 11 students
seniors	8	24	2	6	30

÷4

d.

		x2		÷5	÷2	
tax	1.12	2.24	.28	.056	.028	2.24 + .28 + .028 = $2.55
purchase	$20	40	5	1	.50	$45.50

÷4

e.

	x3		÷2	
US dollars	4.50	13.50	.75	.375	13.50 -.375 = $13.13
Australian dollars	6	18	1	.50	17.50

÷6

13. Student A used a correct strategy. Notice that after removing one copy of 3:4 from 5:8, you are left with 2:4, which is less than 3:4. Student B used a correct strategy, but did not know how to interpret the result. Because there are 2 "against" dots remaining, 3:4< 5:6. We get 0:2 and conclude that 5:6 > 2:3 although there were 3 copies of 5:6 and 5 copies of 3:4. Student C used a correct strategy. You can check using ratio arithmetic. $5(7:9) = 35:45$. $7(5:8) = 35:56$. $35:45 - 35:56 = 0:-11$.

Chapter 12
Analyzing Change

1. a. Changing quantities include the amount of gas in your tank, the number of gallons registered on the gas pump, the price registered on the gas pump, and time.
b. Changing quantities include time, distance from your starting point, amount of gas in your tank, your speed, and amount of gas consumed by your car.
c. Changing quantities include shopping time, the amount of each purchase, and your total credit card bill.
d. Changing quantities include amount of time since you started, your depth or distance from the surface, pressure, amount of air in your tank, and the amount of sunlight reaching you.
e. Changing quantities include time and volume of water in the tub.

2. The amount of money put into the machine changed; time changed; the ratio 2 dimes and 1 nickel:1 quarter did not change.

3. The number of piles changed; the number of light chips in each pile changed; the number of dark chips in each pile changed; time changed. The relationship between the number of light chips and the number of dark chips in each pile did not change.

4. Time changed. The creatures each ate a different number of meals, but the number of food pellets for each per meal did not change.

5. The size of the skull changed, but the shape of the skull did not change.

6. The number of tables in each group changed; the number of students per table changed. The number of candy bars did not change, and so the amount of candy person did not change. Everyone will get $\frac{3}{4}$ of a candy bar.

7. a. The cost of getting into the park depends on the number of people in your family.
b. The reading on your car's odometer does not depend on how fast you are going. The odometer measures distance; the speedometer measures speed.
c. Time spent traveling depends on the distance you need to travel as well as how fast you are going, and distance traveled depends on the amount of time traveled at a particular speed.
d. No dependence.

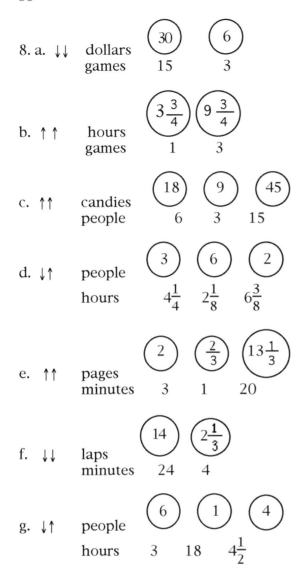

8. a. ↓↓   dollars   30   6
            games   15   3

b. ↑↑   hours $3\frac{3}{4}$ $9\frac{3}{4}$
         games   1   3

c. ↑↑   candies   18   9   45
         people   6   3   15

d. ↓↑   people   3   6   2
         hours $4\frac{1}{4}$ $2\frac{1}{8}$ $6\frac{3}{8}$

e. ↑↑   pages   2 $\frac{2}{3}$ $13\frac{1}{3}$
         minutes 3   1   20

f. ↓↓   laps   14 $2\frac{1}{3}$
         minutes 24   4

g. ↓↑   people   6   1   4
         hours   3   18 $4\frac{1}{2}$

9. a. ↑↑ correct

b. The time the cruise takes does not depend on the number of people aboard.

c. ↓↑   If the number of people decreases, the time to do the job increases. It will take 3 people 2 hours to clean it.

d. ↑↓ If the number of people doing the job increases, it will take less time to do the job. Two boys could mow the lawn in $1\frac{1}{2}$ hours.

e. You cannot correct this statement. Families have different numbers of children.

f. ↑↓ correct

g. The time it takes to play the symphony does not depend on how many orchestras are playing together.

10. a. periodic
b. decreasing
c. increasing
d. irregular
e. periodic
f. increasing

11. a. The cost of printing x calendars is 3.25 for each calendar (3.25x) + the 850 base fixed price.

$$\text{Cost} = 3.25\,x + 850$$

b. The average cost is the cost divided by the total number of calendars.

$$AC = \frac{3.25\ x\ +\ 850}{x}$$

c. As the number of calendars increases, the average cost decreases.
    ↑↓

d. Arrange the numbers of calendars and the average costs you have calculated for each of those quantities in a table.

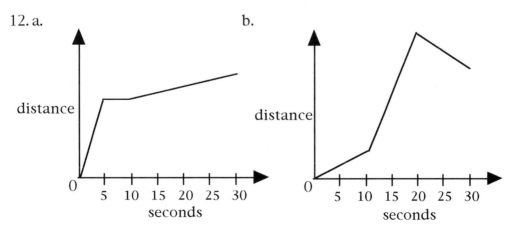

Number	Average Cost
10	$88.25
100	$11.75
500	$ 4.95
1000	$ 4.10

You can see that when the number is multiplied by 10, the average cost is multiplied by $\frac{1}{7.51}$ ($88.25 ÷ 11.75). When the number is multiplied by 100, the average cost is multiplied by $\frac{1}{21.52}$. Thus, the average cost decreases more slowly than the size of your order increases.

12. a.   b.

c.

d.

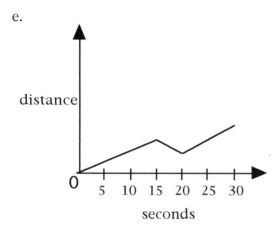

e.

13. a. This person rested for the first 10 seconds then ran for 20 seconds.
b. This person ran for 10 seconds, rested for 5 seconds, then ran faster for 5 seconds and rested again.
c. This graph does not depict an actual situation because it shows that the person was always in two places at the same time.
d. This person ran for 10 seconds and then walked for 20 seconds.
e. This person ran for 15 seconds, ran even faster for the next 5 seconds, then turned around and ran to the starting point.
f. This graph is impossible because it shows that, at times, a person would have to be in three places at once.

14.

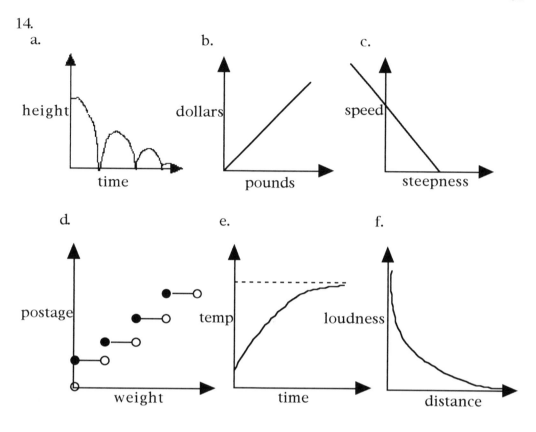

a.   height / time

b.   dollars / pounds

c.   speed / steepness

d.   postage / weight

e.   temp / time

f.   loudness / distance

15. a. Time decreases more slowly than number increases.
b. Stopping distance increases more quickly than speed increases.
c. At first, the amount of water decreases more rapidly, then, toward the end, decreases more slowly.
d. The two quantities change at the same rate.
e. The number of years increases more rapidly than the diameter of the tree.
f. At first, the time decreases more rapidly than the speed increases, but later, the speed increases more rapidly than the time.

a.   b.   c.

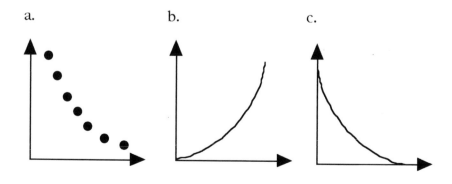

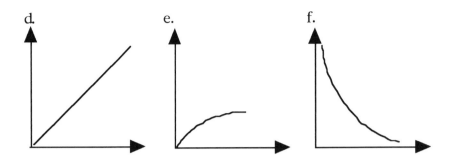

Chapter 13
Rates

1. a. $\dfrac{4 \ \text{teaspoons}}{6 \ \text{ounces}} = \dfrac{8 \ (\frac{1}{2}\text{-teaspoons})}{12 \ (\frac{1}{2}\text{-ounces})}$ and $\dfrac{3 \ \text{teaspoons}}{4 \ \text{ounces}} = \dfrac{9 \ (\frac{1}{3}\text{-teaspoons})}{12 \ (\frac{1}{3}\text{-ounces})}.$

Today's mixture is more chocolaty.

b. $\dfrac{\$15 \ \text{taxes}}{\$68 \ \text{spent}} = \dfrac{3(\$5 \ \text{in} \ \text{taxes})}{13\frac{3}{5}(\$5 \ \text{spent})}$ and $\dfrac{\$12 \ \text{taxes}}{\$52 \ \text{spent}} = \dfrac{3(\$4 \ \text{taxes})}{13(\$4 \ \text{spent})},$ so $15 tax on a

$68 purchase is a cheaper tax rate.

2. a. 380 miles in 6 hours is equivalent to 63.33 mph or $\dfrac{63.33 \ \text{miles}}{1 \ \text{hour}}.$
565 miles in 9 hours is equivalent to 62.78 mph. Greg's average speed was slower.
b. Stacy's offered 15% or $15 off on $100. The unit rate of discount is $\dfrac{1}{6.67}.$ Boss Store's unit rate of discount was $\dfrac{1}{5}.$ Boss Store offered the better discount.

3. a.

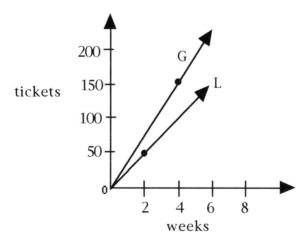

The graph show tickets sold per weeks and the steeper of the graphs shows the equivalence class for the Globe. The Globe is selling tickets at a faster rate.

b.

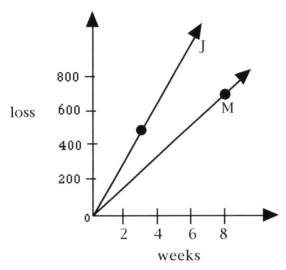

The graph shows losses per week. The Jones Company has the steeper graph, thus indicating that they are losing more quickly. The McDuff Company is losing less rapidly.

c.

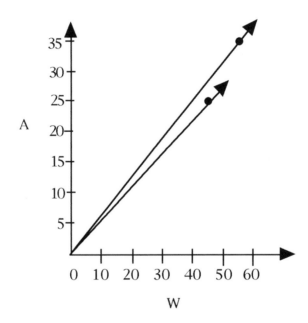

The solution of 35 parts ammonia to 55 parts water is stronger, corresponding to the steeper line on the graph.

4. Your average increase over 3 years was $.83 per hour.

5. a. The change is 24 miles in 29 minutes or $\frac{29}{60}$ hour. $24 \div \frac{29}{60} = 49.66$ mph.

b. 73.13 mph

c. 61.97 mph, or about 62 mph

6. $\dfrac{\$4.50}{1 \text{ pound}} = \dfrac{\$.50}{\frac{1}{9} \text{ pound}} = \dfrac{\$1.00}{\frac{2}{9} \text{ pound}}$

7. a. Find the total distance around the track (mi or km) covered by each driver by counting how many times he went around and divide by the time (3 hours) to get each driver's speed (mph or kph).

b. Time the drivers to see how long it took them to drive the 50 km and then divide that distance (km) by time (hours) to get km. per hour.

8. a. After 10 minutes, B was ahead of A and stayed in the lead throughout the hour.

b. In 60 minutes, B covered 6 miles. B's rate was 6 mph. A covered 2 miles in 60 minutes. A's rate was 2 mph.

c. When you divide the total distance covered by the total time it took, you get average speed. So 6 mph and 2 mph are average speeds. Typically, knowing an average speed does not tell us what rate a person was moving in any particular interval. They could be moving a little faster in one interval and a little slower in the next. However, in this case, because A's and B's positions in the sketch are in a straight line, we know that each kept the same pace throughout the 60 minutes.

9. It took 15 minutes. The distance (7 miles) divided by the rate (28 mph) gives a time of $\frac{1}{4}$ hour.

10. The average speed was 21 mph. The distance (7 miles) divided by the time it took to go that distance (20 minutes or $\frac{1}{3}$ hr.) gives 21 mph.

11. $\frac{1}{5}$ mi. in 10 seconds = $\frac{1}{50}$ mi. per second = $\frac{60}{50}$ mi. per min. = $\frac{3600}{50}$ mi. per hour = 72 mph.

12. 32 beats per 15 seconds = 128 beats per minute.

13. a. 40 km in 3 hours = $13\frac{1}{3}$ kph.

b. 20 km in 2 hours = 10 kph.

c. 60 km in 5 hours = 12 kph

14. Charlie could have argued that his average speed was under the speed limit. For the first 5 miles, he drove 80 mph, which took him .0625

hr. (3.75 minutes). For the next 5 miles, he drove 40 mph, which took him .125 hr. (7.5 minutes). His average speed was the total distance divided by the total time or 10 ÷ .1875 hr.= 53.33 mph.

15. The distance between the cities does not change; the distance one way is the same as the distance the other way. Suppose that distance is d. Then d ÷ 50 mph is the time it took Frank to drive to Washington and d ÷ 60 is the time it took him to drive back to Boston. The total of those times is 18 hours, so

$$\frac{d}{50} + \frac{d}{60} = 18 \text{ hours}$$
$$\frac{6d+5d}{300} = 18 \text{ hours}$$
$$11d = 5400 \text{ mi.}$$
$$d = 490.91 \text{ mi.}$$

16. Remember that the cruise ship keeps moving, so even if the speedboat can travel at a rate of 45 knots, it can catch up by a speed of only 20 knots. If the ship had been gone for 2 hours, it had traveled a distance of 50 nautical miles, so to catch up, it would take the speedboat $2\frac{1}{2}$ hours. So at a speed of 45 knots for $2\frac{1}{2}$ hours, the speedboat would meet the ship at a distance of 112.5 nautical miles from the dock. the ship would have gone $4\frac{1}{2}$ hours at 25 $\frac{\text{knots}}{\text{hour}}$, the same distance.

17. The twins were traveling toward each other at 20 mph and they were 10 miles apart. That means one twin alone could travel the distance in $\frac{1}{2}$ hour, and since they were splitting that distance, it would take them only $\frac{1}{4}$ hour. Therefore, Frieda flew $50 \cdot \frac{1}{4} = 12.5$ miles.

18. If t is the time it takes the bikes to meet, then 10t represents the distance Frank traveled and 8t represents the distance Flo traveled. The distance between them was 9 km, so 10t + 8t = 9 km and t = $\frac{1}{2}$ hour. How far did Free-To Fly fly in $\frac{1}{2}$ hour? At 15 kph, he traveled $7\frac{1}{2}$ km.

19. If I walk 36 steps instead of 26 steps, a difference of 8 steps, I save 12 seconds. This means that for each step, I save $1\frac{1}{2}$ seconds. The steps must be descending at the rate of 1 step in $1\frac{1}{2}$ seconds. Walking 26 steps and riding for 30 seconds is then equivalent to 26 + 20 steps = 46 steps. Similarly, moving 34 steps + 18 seconds translates into 34 + 12 = 46 steps.

20. Walking takes three times as long as traveling by bus. In 8 hours, there are 4 time periods, each 2 hours long, so we need 2 hours of time on the bus, and 6 hours (3 times as long) to walk back. Riding for 2 hours at the rate of 9 mph on the bus, we can go 18 miles.

21. At 10:30, the candles were the same in height. Because the candles burned from the same height in $1\frac{1}{2}$ and 2 hours, respectively, the longer candle burned at $\frac{3}{4}$ the rate of the shorter candle. If R is the rate at which the shorter candle burns, then the total height of the shorter candle is 3R and the total height of the taller is $4\frac{1}{2}$ $(\frac{3}{4}R)$. The taller candle was $1\frac{1}{2}"$ taller than the shorter, so $3R + 1\frac{1}{2}" = 4\frac{1}{2}$ $(\frac{3}{4}R)$. Solving for the rate, $R = 4\frac{inches}{hour}$ for the shorter candle. So the longer candle burned at a rate of $3\frac{inches}{hour}$. This means that the height of the taller candle was $13\frac{1}{2}$ inches and the height of the shorter candle was 12 inches.

22. Jim can cut $\frac{1}{4}$ lawn in 1 hour. His brother can cut $\frac{1}{3}$ lawn in 1 hour. Working together, in 1 hour the boys can cut $\frac{1}{4}$ lawn $+ \frac{1}{3}$ lawn $= \frac{7}{12}$ lawn. This means that they can cut $\frac{1}{12}$ lawn in $\frac{1}{7}$ hour, and the whole lawn in $\frac{12}{7}$ hours $= 1\frac{5}{7}$ hours $= 1$ hour and 43 minutes.

23. a. There are 130 km between stations A and D.
b. The hound has to run 75 meters to catch up to the fox.
c. The second worker makes 14 parts and hour.

Chapter 14
Reasoning Proportionally

1. a. If three pints cost $1.59, then 1 pint should cost $.53 ($\frac{1}{3}$ as much) and 4 should cost $2.12 (4 times the cost of 1). The milk cartons are priced proportionally. Another way to think about it: Are both ratios in the same equivalence class? Check the divided ratios. $\frac{2.12}{4} = \frac{.53}{1}$ and $\frac{1.59}{3} = \frac{.53}{1}$.

b.   This situation does not involve proportional or inversely proportional relationships. How long it takes to drive to the basketball game has nothing to do with how many people are in the car.

c. The number of people is cut in half, which means that the work should take twice as long. This is the case, and the situation involves an inversely proportional relationship between number of people and time it takes to do a job.

d.   This situation does not involve any proportional or inversely proportional relationships. The number of sisters one boy has has nothing to do with how many sisters another boy has.

e.   This situation does not involve any proportional or inversely proportional relationships. Time spent on solving a problem is not really dependent on where a person is solving it.

f. If number of eggs and time to eat them are proportional, then it should take 20 times as long to eat 20 eggs as it does to eat one egg. However, this is not the case.   1 egg per 20 seconds = 3 eggs per minute. The average rate for eating 20 eggs was 4 eggs per minute.

g. Gallons of gas and distance traveled are proportionally related. A full tank of gas (15 gallons) is 3.33333 times 4.5 gallons and 333 miles is 3.33333 times 100 miles, the distance traveled on 4.5 gallons.

h. Amount spent and sales tax are proportionally related. When you spent $35 and paid $2.10 in sales tax, you spent 7 times as much as when you spent $5 and paid 7 times what you paid on sales tax.

2.
a.

	# tickets	profit	notes
a	1	$1.15	given
b	100	115	100a
c	10	11.50	10a
d	5	5.75	.5c
e	20	23	2c
f	3	3.45	3a
g	128	147.20	b+d+e+f

The school makes $147.20 on 128 tickets.

b.

	# cans	cost	notes
a	1	$4.49	given
b	10	44.90	10a
c	5	22.45	.5b
d	15	67.35	b+c

There is enough money to buy 15 cans.

c.

	distance (km)	time (min)	notes
a	10	45	given
b	1	4.5	a÷10
c	6	27	6b
d	.1	.45	b÷10
e	.2	.90	2d
f	.01	.045	d÷10
g	.05	.225	5f
h	6.25	28.125	c+e+g

It would take him just a little over 28 minutes.

3. a. 2875 words.
b. $38.99.
c. 8 baseball caps.
d. $414\frac{3}{8}$ miles.
e. $45.
f. 9.8 quarts.

4. a. Not a proportional relationship.

Diameter (feet)	Area (sq. ft.)
3	7.06858
6	28.27433

x 2 (left, between 3 and 6)   x 4 (right, between 7.06858 and 28.27433)

b. Not a proportional relationship.

distance (miles)	cost (dollars)
2	5.50
10	21.50
50	101.50

x 5 (between 2 and 10)   x 3.91 (between 5.50 and 21.50)
x 5 (between 10 and 50)   x 4.72 (between 21.50 and 101.50)

c. There is a proportional relationship between the length and perimeter.

Length (feet)	Perimeter (feet)
3	9
9	27

x 3 (between 3 and 9)   x 3 (between 9 and 27)

P = 3L

5. Hold the number of men constant and figure how long it would take them to cut 3 cords. Then hold the cords constant and find the amount of time it would take half as many men to cut them.

men	8	8	4
cords	9	3	3
hours	6.5	2.1666	4.3333

6. Hold the time constant and figure out how many cars 14 robots can make. Then hold the robots constant and figure out how many cars they can make in 8 hours.

robots	3	12	1	2	14	14	14
cars	19	76	6.333	12.666	88.666	8.866	17
hours	40	40	40	40	40	4	8

7. It took the car 29 of Sam's steps to go as far as Sam went in 203 steps. $\frac{203}{29} = 7$. Therefore the car was moving 7 times as fast as Sam. Since Sam was walking $3\frac{1}{2}$ mph, the car must have been going $24\frac{1}{2}$ mph.

8. a. There is a proportional relationship between weight in pounds and weight in kilograms. In both of the instances given, the ratio of pounds to kilograms is 2.20. We can express this in the equation p = 2.2 k.

b. There is a proportional relationship between the striking distance and the time until you hear the crash. The time at which the crash is heard is three times the distance from where the lightening struck. We can express this in the equation t = 3d.

c. There is a proportional relationship between the pressure on your ears and your distance under the water. The pressure is .43 times the distance. We can express this in the equation p = .43 d.

9. a. 1 horse will eat 15 pounds of hay.
b. 10 robots will produce 600 packages of auto parts in 10 hours.
c. At the same rate, 24 hens will produce 384 eggs or 32 dozen eggs in 24 days.

Chapter 15
Applications

1. Reposition the triangles so that their right angles are on a coordinate graph at (0,0). If the triangles are similar, their third sides should be parallel. Look at triangle whose coordinates are (0,4) and (3,0). Its third side is parallel to the third side of the largest triangle. This means that the ratios y:x = 8:6 = 4:3, which are also the slope of the third sides, are all the same.

2. a. The ratio of a side of the larger square to the side of the smaller square is 8:2 = 4:1.

b. The scale factor is $\frac{1}{4}$.

3. a. The second is half the size of the first.

b. The scale factor is $\frac{1}{2}$.

c. Right angles stayed the same.
d. Vertical segments became half as long.
e. Horizontal segments became half as long.
f. Diagonal segments became half as long.

g. The area of the smaller circle is $\frac{1}{4}$ the area of the larger.

h. The area of the smaller square is $\frac{1}{4}$ the area of the larger.

i. Shrinking or enlarging multiplies each length by the scale factor and each area by the scale factor times itself.

4. Books: yes.
Cats, no; they did not shrink in all dimensions (heads, necks, tails, feet are the same in both pictures).
Trees, yes.
Trucks, no; the trucks have different cabs and different numbers of wheels.

5. Compare the areas to the prices of the pizzas.

area (sq. in.)	price
78.54	$6.80
113.1	8.50
153.94	13.60
314.16	28.00

a. Compare price to number of square inches. For the 10' pizza, you pay $.086 a square inch; for the 12" pizza, $.075 a square inch; for the 14" pizza, $.088 a square inch; for the 20" pizza, $.089 a square inch. The 12" pizza looks like the best buy.

b. The pizzas are not priced proportionally. 78.54 sq. in. doubled is less than 153.94 sq. in., but the price for 153.94 sq. in. is double the price for 78.54 sq. in.

6. a. A smaller triangle similar to triangle ABC can be made simply by drawing a line parallel to side BC. The new triangle (named triangle APE below) is similar to triangle ABC. To show this, find the ratios $\frac{AP}{AB}, \frac{AE}{AC}, \frac{PE}{BC}$. They should all be the same. There are many places where you could have drawn PE. However, for the example given here,

m(AP) = 1.125 and m(AB) = 2.25. $\frac{AP}{AB}$ = .5.

m(AE) = .875 and m(AC)= 1.75 $\frac{AE}{AC}$ = .5

m(PE) = .75 and m(BC) = 1.5 $\frac{PE}{BC}$ = .5

The scale factor is .5.

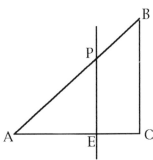

b. By measuring sides BC and AC, you can find the slope of side AB, $\frac{1.5}{1.75}$. Scaling up, say, by a factor of 10, we get a triangle whose legs BC and AC measure 15 and 17.5, respectively.

7. A ratio of 1:1 means that the rectangles are squares.

8. The ratio of length to width in a square is 1:1 because all sides are the same length. So the rectangle whose ratio of sides is closest to 1 will be closest to being square. Taking the ratio of shorter to longer sides, we get $\frac{5.5}{7.8}$ = .705 and $\frac{6.25}{8.7}$ = .718. This means that rectangle B is closer to being square. If we had taken the ratios of longer to shorter sides, we would get $\frac{7.8}{5.5}$ = 1.42 and $\frac{8.7}{6.25}$ = 1.39. The ratio for rectangle B is closer to 1.

9. Three groups of rectangles.
A. 2 x 6, 5 x 15, 6 x 18
B. 3 x 6, 4 x 8, 7 x 14, 11 x 22
C. 8 x 12, 10 x 15, 12 x 18

10. The smaller figure measures 2 units by 2 units. The larger figure measures 4 units by 2 units. One dimension doubled and the other stayed the same. These are not similar figures. All dimensions must increase by the same factor.

11.
a. The original mast must have been $(2.5)(14) = 35$ ' tall.

b. The original fish must have been $80 \, (\frac{1}{25}) = 3.2$ feet long.

c. The original area must have been $(25)(\frac{1}{4.5})(\frac{1}{4.5}) = 1.235$ sq. ft.

12.
a. 25% of 80 = 20

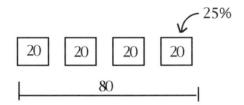

b. 15 = 30% of 50

c. 45 = 75% of 60

d. 14 = 20% of 70

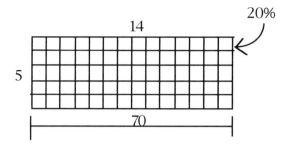

e. 65% of 90 = 58.5

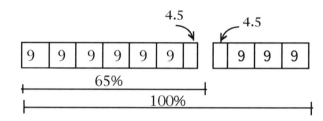

f. 28 = 40% of 70

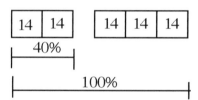

g. 15% of 80 = 12

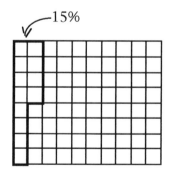

h. 36 is 40% of 90

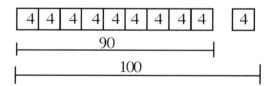

i. 27 is 45% of _____

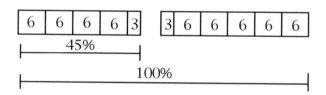

13. a. 20
b. 80
c. 60
d. 4
e. 24
f. 104
g. 2
h. 6
i. 22
j. 14

14. The markup is the amount of money the bookstore charges the student above and beyond what the store paid for the book. The equation says that the cost to the bookstore is $\frac{3}{4}$ what the student pays (C $=\frac{3}{4}$ S). This means that the student pays $\frac{4}{3}$ times the cost to the bookstore. So the markup is $\frac{1}{3}$ the cost to the bookstore or $33\frac{1}{3}$%.

15. a. If there were 100 questions, 80% would be 80 questions, so if there are only 50 questions, 80% is 40 correct.

b. 10% would be $1,500, so 5% is $750.

c. 1% would be $18, so 8% would be 8 times as much, or $144.

d. 10% is 20 pounds and 5% is 10 pounds, so the 15% that is not water weighs 30 pounds. The water must weigh 170 pounds.

16.
a.

%	100	50	10	1	2	62
#	30	15	3	.3	.6	18.6

b.

%	100	10	30	1	6	136
#	80	8	24	.8	4.8	108.8

c.

%	100	50	5	1	7	57
#	29	14.5	1.45	.29	2.03	16.53

17.

  a.   b.   c.

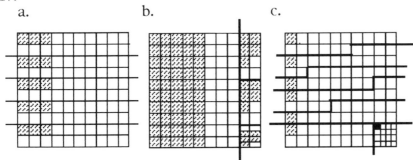

18. To enlarge, each dimension must increase by the same factor. 3.5"(2.286) = 8", but 5"(2.2) = 11". Because you cannot increase both dimensions by the same factor, it will not be a true enlargement. Some of the original picture will get cut off when it is enlarged to fit on $8\frac{1}{2}$" x 11" paper.

Part II
Supplementary Activities

Chapter 2
Relative and Absolute Thinking

1.

How many more stars are there in box B than in box A?
How many times the number of stars in A are in B?
How many times the number of stars in B are in A?
Set A is what part of set B?
If there are two stars in a group, how many groups did it take to make box A? box B?

2. Can you tell by looking at the following pools which one has a greater capacity? Which pool has the greater area? In addition to the area, what quantity is needed to describe capacity? By choosing appropriate depths for each of the pools, show that sometimes the first pool might have the greater capacity, and sometimes the second might have the greater capacity.

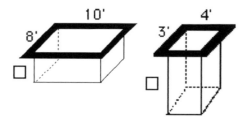

3. Today there is a sale at Neville's Women's Shop: $10.00 off the sticker price of every item! Describe exactly how you can tell which is a better buy, a dress marked $44.99 or a blouse marked $26.99.

4. What kind of information is necessary to describe the "orangyness" of a drink?

5. Think of other examples in which the comparison of two quantities are needed to describe a certain characteristic of the situation.

6. What does it mean to say that a grasshopper can jump relatively higher than a person can?

7. The Manhattan Mercury reported that in 1950, when there was a population of 19,000 people, there were 12 people per acre in the city of Manhattan, Kansas. By 1995, when the population was 43,000, there

were only 5 people per acre.   Interpret this information as completely
as possible.

8.   There were 7 males and 12 females in the Dew Drop Inn on Monday
night.   In the Game Room next door, there were 14 males and 24 females.
Which spot had more females?

9.   Investigation: Shrinking and Enlarging
You will need some graph paper.
a.   Plot the vertices of a square or rectangle.
b.   Add 2 to each of the coordinates of each vertex of your figure.
c.   Plot and connect the resulting points on the same graph.
d.   Multiply the coordinates of each of your original vertices by 2.
e.   Plot and connect the resulting points on the same graph.
f.   What does this investigation show?   State your results precisely.

Chapter 3
Fractions and Rational Numbers

1. What operation is suggested by this problem: $\frac{2}{3}$ of a liter of juice costs $1.89. At the same rate, what is the price per liter?

2. John took one step and it measured .75 meters long. Would it take more than 10 or fewer than 10 steps to measure a distance of 10 meters? Why? What operation does this problems suggest?

3. What operation is suggested by this problem? You went to the deli counter to buy some lunchmeat. It was on sale for $4.29 per pound. The person at the counter piled the sliced meat on the scale until you indicated that you had enough. At that point, the meter read .94 pounds. How much should you pay for the meat?

4. What operation is suggested by the following problem? The exchange rate today is $1.84 dollars per British pound ($£$). Excluding transaction charges, how many pounds can you get for $500?

5. The Terrific Toy Company received a total of 240 model cars in 3 huge cartons with 10 boxes per carton. How many cars were in each box? What operation can be used to solve this problem? Write a mathematical statement to solve this problem, being careful to label each quantity appropriately.

6. Is $\frac{1}{3}$ of a 3-unit the same as 3 one-third units? Draw pictures and explain.

7. Is one 12-unit the same as four 3-units? Draw pictures and explain.

Chapter 4
Units and Unitizing

1. Specify the unit defined implicitly in each of the following examples. Do not do any writing. Explain your reasoning aloud.

a.  is $1\frac{2}{3}$.

b. 3 orks + 2 orks = . Find $1\frac{2}{3}$ orks.

c. ☆☆☆☆ is $\frac{1}{5}$. Find $\frac{3}{4}$.

d. 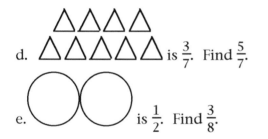 is $\frac{3}{7}$. Find $\frac{5}{7}$.

e. ◯◯ is $\frac{1}{2}$. Find $\frac{3}{8}$.

2. Comment on this picture:

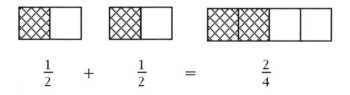

$$\frac{1}{2} \quad + \quad \frac{1}{2} \quad = \quad \frac{2}{4}$$

3. Tim spent $\frac{1}{4}$ of his money, and Pete spent half of his. Is it possible that Tim spent more money than John?

4. Draw $2\frac{3}{5}$ packs of Yum Gum. Draw $2\frac{1}{4}$ times as many hard candies as shown.

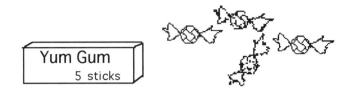

What are the differences between using the hard candies as a unit and using the pack of gum as a unit?

5. Generate as many names as you can for $1\frac{1}{2}$ recs. Use Rec 1.

6. Using Rec 3, create three questions whose answers are fractions whose numerators are smaller than their denominators. Give the answers.

7. Unitize each quantity in at least two different ways:
a. 3 weeks =
b. $.05 =
c. 16 (half pints) =
d. $1\frac{1}{2}$ dozen =
e. 26 (quarter-miles) =
f. 3 inches =
g. 5 (5-packs) of gum =
h. 17 pairs of shoelaces =
i. 3 (8-packs) of soda =

Chapter 5
Part-Whole Comparisons

1. If the number of dogs is $\frac{5}{3}$ the number of cats in the town of Rosedale, are there fewer cats or fewer dogs in the town? Draw a picture to show the answer. What is the unit? How many times the smaller group is the larger group?

2. One row of seats holds 12 people. What part of a row will four couples occupy? Suppose we define a "quad" as a group of 4 people. What part—whole comparison do you get using quads? Draw pictures to show that it represents the same comparison as when you use single people and couples to determine part of a row.

3. 10 cents is what part of a dollar? Find 3 different ways to name the part of a dollar.

4. What part of the surface area of a cube is the area of 1 face of the cube?

5. What part of 2^5 is 2^2?

6. Use unitizing to determine what part of this set of diamonds you circle to designate $\frac{3}{5}$.

7. How can you decide how many to circle if you want $\frac{7}{10}$ of the group of diamonds in # 6?

8. Use unitizing to compare the following fractions: $\frac{5}{6}$, $\frac{7}{8}$, and $\frac{11}{12}$ in relation to this set:

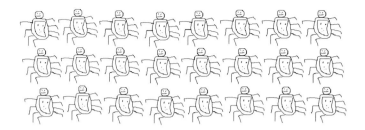

Chapter 6
Partitioning and Quotients

1. Two children shared a candy bar and one was crying and screaming, "Your half is bigger than my half!" Why was the child was upset? What did he mean?

2. Alice and Brad will share a large cookie. Is there a way to partition the cookie so that one child gets two pieces and the other child gets three pieces, but they both get the same amount?

3. Stacy gave the following solution to question #11. Is she correct?

4. Three people share the following candy bars. Show three different partitions, write the fractions to represent the pieces in each share, and note the equivalencies:

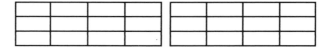

5. Do these partitions show fourths or not? Explain why or why not.

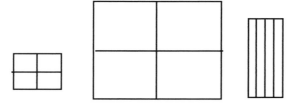

6. If 3 people share these candy bars, how much will one share be? What part of the unit is each share?

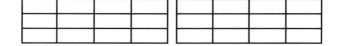

7. Eight people share 6 cheese and 4 mushroom pizzas. How much of each type of pizza is in a share? How much of the total pizza does each person get?

8. Suppose three girls share 3 pepperoni pizzas and 4 cheese pizzas. How much will each person get? If each of them takes her portion home and later shares it with her sister, how much will each girl eat? What part of the total amount of pizza will each girl eat?

9. Look back at the problem in this chapter in which $\frac{5}{8}$-yard pieces were cut from a 6-yard piece of rope. Would you ask students this question: What part of the original length of rope is each share?

10. Draw a picture to solve this problem: If package of macaroni contains $15\frac{1}{2}$ ounces and the suggested serving is $3\frac{1}{4}$ ounces per person, how many people will the package serve? How many servings are in the package?

11. Draw a picture to solve this problem: The Fleet-of-Foot Track Team will enter some of its members in an upcoming relay race that is $3\frac{1}{5}$ miles long. The coach has determined that his runners do best in $\frac{3}{4}$ -mile stretches. How many runners will he need for the relay race? What part of a stretch will the last runner do?

12. In the macaroni problem (#10), what part of the package is each serving? What part of the package is the partial serving?

Chapter 7
Rational Numbers as Operators

1. Reducing a unit to half its size and then tripling the result in size is equivalent to _____.

2. Dividing something into 5 equal shares and then quadrupling each share is equivalent to _____.

3. Describe in symbols what happens in the pictures:

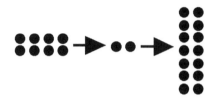

4. Make a picture showing a two-for-three operator with an input of 12 items and another picture of an eight-for-twelve operator with an input of 12 items. Predict some other exchangers that will yield the same result.

5. Use an area model to do the following multiplications:

a. $\frac{2}{5} \times \frac{5}{6}$

b. $\frac{2}{3} \times \frac{3}{4}$

c. $1\frac{1}{2} \times \frac{1}{3}$

6. Draw a picture to illustrate the action of a 2-for-8 operator on a 4-for-3 operator on this set of objects:

7. What conclusions can you draw about the operators and their relative sizes, given the following machines?

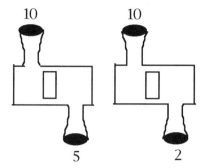

8. Use an area model to do the following divisions:

a. $1\frac{1}{2} \div \frac{3}{4}$

b. $1\frac{1}{3} \div 2$

9. Find the number of children who are girls if you know that there are 12 male adults.

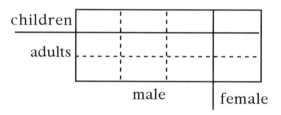

10. Try this investigation.

Fold one unit sheet of paper into thirds. Shade $\frac{1}{3}$.

Fold another unit of the same size into fourths. Shade $\frac{1}{4}$.

Fold each of the units into twelfths.
Open each unit and express the shaded amounts in twelfths.
What conclusions can you draw?

11. Fold two paper units until you can rename each of these fractions with the same denominator:

$$\frac{3}{8} \text{ and } \frac{1}{6}$$

12. Complete each diagram and carry out the paper folding that will result in the smallest fraction.

a.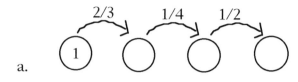

b.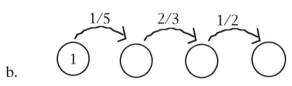

Chapter 8
Rational Numbers as Measures

1. Today was your lucky day. You found a parking meter that had lots of time on it. How much time do you have?

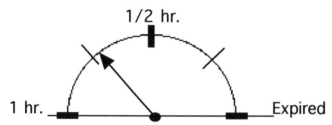

2. You need about $\frac{1}{2}$ hour to return something at the department store downtown. You pull into a parking meter that has just a little time left on it. The meter indicates that 1 nickel buys 3 minutes of time, for 1 dime, you get 8 minutes, and for 1 quarter, you get 20 minutes. What is the least amount of money you should deposit?

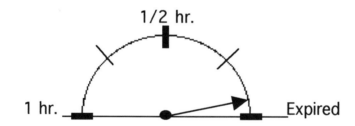

3. In each case, show the length of the unit interval.

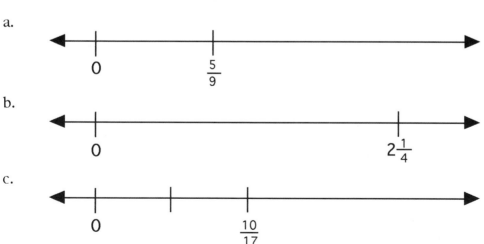

4. Parking downtown is expensive. The meters indicate that 1 nickel buys 3 minutes of time, for 1 dime, you get 8 minutes, and for 1 quarter, you get 20 minutes. You put in 2 nickels and 4 dimes. Draw an arrow to show how much time registers on the meter.

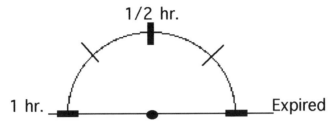

5. a. (A,B) is $\frac{2}{3}$ the unit interval. Locate point X so that the measure of (A,X) is $1\frac{1}{4}$ unit intervals.

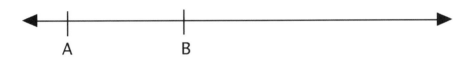

b. (C,D) is $1\frac{1}{15}$ units intervals. Locate point Y so that the measure of (C,Y) is $\frac{7}{30}$ of the unit interval.

c. (E,F) is $2\frac{1}{3}$ unit intervals. Locate point Z so that the measure of (E,Z) is $3\frac{5}{9}$ unit intervals.

d. (G,H) is $\frac{11}{15}$ of a unit interval. Locate point W so that the measure of (G,W) is $1\frac{3}{5}$ unit intervals.

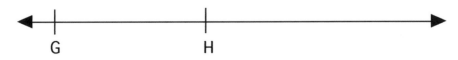

6. You and a friend both parked your cars downtown while you shopped together. At lunch time, you went out to check your meters. You decided that you would need another $1\frac{1}{2}$ hours. The meters indicate that 1 nickel buys 3 minutes of time, for 1 dime, you get 8 minutes, and for 1 quarter, you get 20 minutes. What is the least amount of money you should put into your meter (a) and what is the least amount of money your friend should put into his meter (b)?

a. your meter

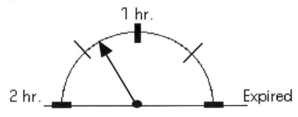

b. your friend's meter

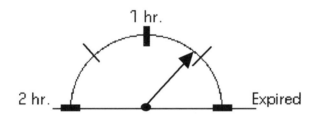

7. By partitioning the interval between the given fractions, find four fractions between them.

a. $\frac{3}{8}$ and $\frac{1}{2}$

b. $\frac{3}{13}$ and $\frac{17}{65}$

Chapter 9
Quantitative Relationships :
Visual and Verbal

1. a. Suppose these wheels each make 3 full turns. Will both wheels cover the same distance? How do you know?
b. Suppose both wheels travel a distance of 1 mile. Will they both make the same number of turns? How do you know?

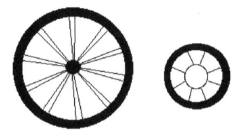

2. Suppose a huge freight train entered this tunnel at the end nearest to you. Would it be able to get out the other end?

3. Tom and Jenny each have a bag of cookies to share with the other students at their tables. Their groups each have three people, and the teacher says you may join either group. If you love cookies, which group will you choose? Why?

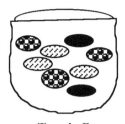

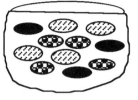

Tom's Bag   Jenny's Bag

4. If Joe is 5 feet tall, how high do you think the building is? How do you know?

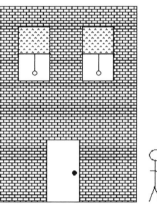

5. [ ] is a 1x1 inch square. Freehand and by eye, without using the square to help you measure, draw a rectangle of each of the following dimensions:

    1 x 2   2 x 2   1 x 3   2 x 3   3 x 3

6. The Perry Pie Company makes mini-pies and sells them in three different-sized packages. Someone forgot to write the price on one of the packages. Can you figure out what it must cost?

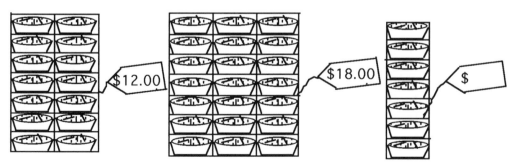

7. Do not measure or overlap these shapes. Do not use any tools. These are to be solved visually.

How many of these ▢ in: ▭

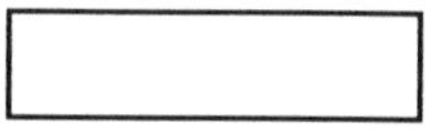

How many of these 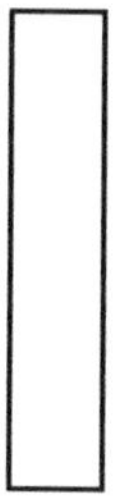 ▯ in: ▢

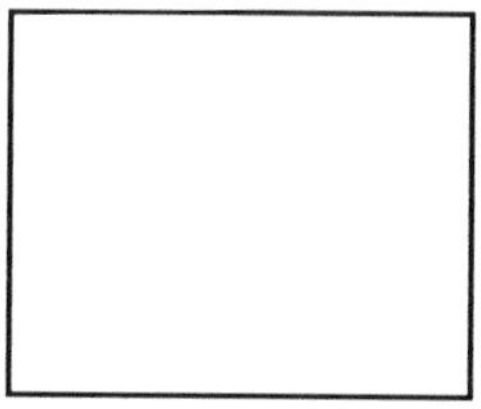

How many of these  △ in: ▱

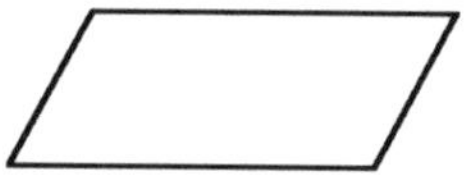

How many of these 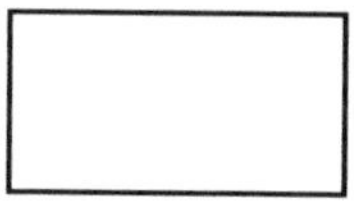 ▭ in: ▢

8. Yesterday, I shared some cookies with some friends. Today I will share my cookies again. Will each person get more, less, or the same amount they got yesterday?

a. Today I have more cookies and the same number of people.
b. Today I have fewer cookies and more people.
c. Today I have the same number of cookies and more people.
d. Today I have more cookies and more people.
e. Today I have fewer cookies and fewer people.
f. Today I have more cookies and fewer people.
g. Today I have the same number of cookies and fewer people.
h. Today I have fewer cookies and the same number of people.

9. In each of the pictures below, the first two blocks define a relationship. Does the second pair show the same relationship as the first pair? If not, replace one of the blocks in the second pair so that you get the same relationship as in the first pair.

a.

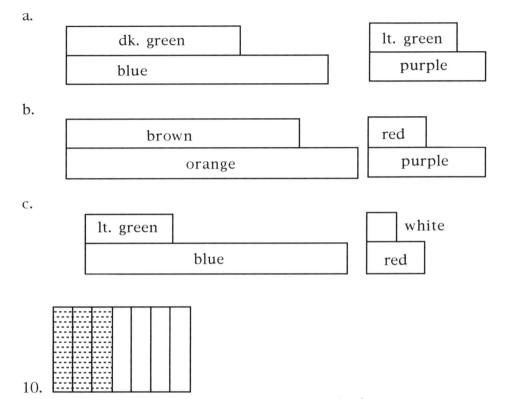

b.

c.

10.

Explain to someone exactly how you can see $\frac{4}{7} \div \frac{3}{7}$.

Chapter 10
Reasoning With Fractions

1. Compare by shading: $\frac{3}{8}$ and $\frac{2}{7}$.

2. Compare the fractions in each pair. Justify your answer using SNP, SSP, or CRP.

a. $\frac{8}{19}, \frac{9}{17}$

b. $\frac{7}{3}, \frac{9}{4}$

c. $\frac{7}{15}, \frac{9}{14}$

3. Use Martin's method to find three fractions between the given fractions.

a. $\frac{1}{14}, \frac{1}{15}$

b. $\frac{14}{5}, 3$

4. How much each bucket hold? H means "holds the same as"

5.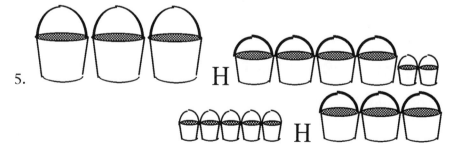

Which hold more:

6 Construct a fraction close to $\frac{1}{2}$. Construct another fraction even closer to $\frac{1}{2}$.

7. Who has more pizza, the girls or the boys?

8. $\frac{2}{9}$ of a class is girls. Are there more girls or more boys? How does the number of boys relate to the number of girls?

9.   There are twice as many boys as girls in my neighborhood.   Are there more girls or more boys? How can you write the relationship between boys and girls?

10. A recipe calls for $\frac{4}{3}$ as much juice as water. Is there more juice or more water? How can you write the relationship between the amount of juice and the amount of water?

11. Jim is $\frac{2}{3}$ as tall as Ted. Who is taller? Express the relationship between their heights.

12. The price of $\frac{2}{3}$ of a liter of juice is $3. Will a liter cost more or less than $3? If the liter is priced at the rate as the $\frac{2}{3}$ liter, what will it cost?

13. My guidebook said that $\frac{2}{3}$ of the population speaks German, $\frac{7}{12}$ speak French, and $\frac{3}{4}$ speak English. I wonder if we will meet some people who speak all three languages.   What is the smallest fraction of the

population that can speak all three languages? What is the largest fraction of the population that can speak all three?

14. Without doing any calculations, put a point on the number line to show approximately where the answer would lie.

a. $1\frac{1}{10} + \frac{7}{8}$

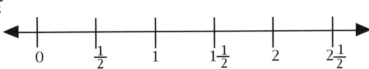

b. $\frac{12}{13} - \frac{3}{7}$

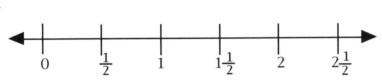

c. $1\frac{4}{7} \times \frac{3}{5}$

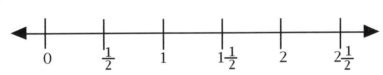

d. $\frac{1}{8} \div 3$

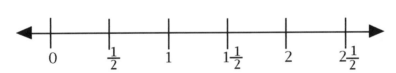

e. $1\frac{1}{4} \div \frac{1}{2}$

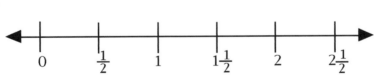

Chapter 11
Ratios

1. Translate these statements into ratio notation:

a. Diet Zoom has $\frac{2}{3}$ fewer calories than the Regular Zoom Cola.

b. Spritzer has $\frac{2}{3}$ as many calories as Splash.

c. The nationally-known brand is half again as expensive as the store brand.

d. For every 2 crooks, there are 300 honest people.

2. Three students from the volleyball team went to Joe's Pizza Place and ordered 2 pizzas. While they were waiting, 3 more students came, so they changed the order to 4 pizzas. More students kept coming into the restaurant, and the team kept ordering more and more pizza so that each person would get the same amount. They ended up buying 15 pizzas. How many players came to the pizza party?

3. At a pizza party, there were 18 pizzas ordered for 24 people. At the restaurant, the people were seated at tables of 4, 6, 6, and 8. How many pizzas should be served to each table so that the pizzas are distributed fairly?

4. Mr. Roberts sent 10 students into the meeting room where there were 6 seats at a large table and 2 small desks. He told them to sit down and wait for him. The boys took all of the seats and left all of the girls standing.
a. What was the ratio of boys to girls?
b. What fraction of the students had seats?
c. What fraction of the students were girls?
d. What was the ratio of students to seats?

5. Sunnybrook Academy reported that their student—teacher ratio was 11:1. The public school in the same area has 624 students.
a. Why does Sunnybrook advertise the ratio 11:1 instead of reporting actual numbers of students and teachers?
b. How many teachers would the public school need to keep up with the academy?

6. Steve compared 3:7 and 6:11 and his dot picture is shown.

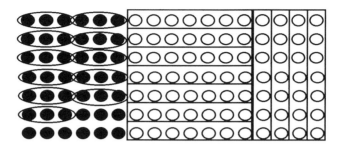

a. What do the 9 uncircled black dots mean?
b. Reinterpret the picture in terms of a ratio subtraction expressed symbolically.

7. Sandra wanted to compare $\frac{3}{4}$ and $\frac{5}{9}$.   She did it by cloning both fractions.
a. Show the dot picture she used and interpret it.
b. Use the dot pictures to write a fraction equation showing the difference between the two fractions.

8. a. Show two different dot pictures comparing 3:4 and 5:9.
b. For each of the pictures, express the difference between the ratios symbolically.

9. Using dot pictures, compare 5:7 and 8:11 two different ways, interpret each solution, and write the ratio subtraction symbolically.

10. Complete each ratio to the right of an arrow, then write the given ratio and a reduced or extended ratio to match each picture.
a.

b.

c.
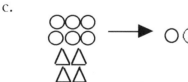

11.   Build a ratio table for each of the following situations:

a. Jack runs $5\frac{3}{8}$ miles a day. What will be his total miles after 117 days?

b. If 2 cm represents a distance of 75 km on my map, how far apart are two cities whose distance on my map is 4 cm + 6 mm?

c. A recipe calls for 2 cups of sugar and $1\frac{1}{4}$ cups of shortening. Mother has only $1\frac{1}{3}$ cups of sugar, so she decides to make a smaller batch. How much shortening will she need?

d. On the average, your car uses $3\frac{1}{2}$ gallons of gas to travel 100 miles. How far can you travel on a full tank of 13 gallons?

12 . Do this investigation.

a. For each point, what is the difference between the x and y coordinates?
(5,1)   (8,4)   (-2, -6)

b. Write an equation to show this difference and graph the equation. On the same axes, graph equations representing constant differences of 0, 2, and 6 between x and y coordinates.

c. Make as many observations as you can about these graphs.

d. Now consider these points: (-2, -4) (2,4) (4,8). How are they different from the first set of points in (a)? For each point, what is the ratio of y to x?

e. Graph the equation $\frac{y}{x} = 2$. On the same axes, graph the equations representing constant ratios of 0, 4, and 6 between x and y.

f. Make as many observations as you can about these graphs.

g. Can you draw a line through (2,4) that does not go through (4,8)?

h. Under what conditions will the line through (2,4) also go through (4,8)?

i. What does ratio have to do with lines through the origin?

Chapter 12
Analyzing Change

In each scenario (1-4), tell which quantities change and which do not change.

1. You set your cruise control and drove for 3 hours without stopping.

2. You puffed into a balloon 3 times every 15 seconds for one minute and the balloon grew larger and larger.

3. You walked at a steady pace all the way from home to school.

4. The skier came down the slope, hitting top speed as she passed the mid-way mark.

5. Teenage Miss Magazine advertises the following ways to subscribe to the magazine.

Term	6 months	9 months	12 months
Cover Price	$30	$45	$60
Your Cost	$27	$40.50	$54

Do you get a better deal if you subscribe for a longer period of time? Explain.

6. Two variable quantities are given in each example. Tell whether one depends on the other. If there is a dependency relationship, which depends on which?

a. Amount of water in the bathtub; how long the water has been running.

b. How many days since you baked bread; how fresh the bread is.

c. Amount of first class postage; weight of a letter.

d. Your age; your height.

7. Some of these statements given are correct; others are not.
Is there a dependency relationship between the important quantities in the situation? If so, use arrow notation to denote the direction of change in each variable. If the statement is incorrect (it does not make sense), change one number in the statement so that it is correct. If you cannot fix the statement, tell why.

a. If 2 books of stamps are worth $11.60, then 3 books should be worth $23.20.

b. If 1 girl can walk to the mall in 20 minutes, then when she walks with her twin sister, the 2 girls should get there in 20 minutes.

c. If 1 basketball player weighs 175 pounds, then 2 players should weigh 350 pounds.

d. If 10 people work on a sewing project, it will take about 4 weeks to complete it, but if 5 people do the work, it will probably take 2 weeks.

e. If it takes Marie about 32 minutes to write 8 party invitations, then it should take her about 40 minutes to write 6 invitations.

f. If it takes 3 brothers 15 minutes to drive to the basketball same game together, then 1 brother could drive to the game by himself in 5 minutes.

g. If 1 man can swim 10 laps in 5 minutes, then 5 men could swim them together in 1 minute.

8. Identify each of the following kinds of change with one of the general categories: increasing, decreasing, periodic, irregular, or stepped. Do not sketch .

a. The height of a yo-yo above the ground changes as you play with it for 10 minutes.
b. The amount of gas in your gas tank changes according to how far you have driven.
c. The price of a box of cereal changes as the volume of the box increases.
d. The amount of money in your paycheck changes according to how many hours you worked.
e. The oceans' tides change over several days.
f. How fast your heart is beating changes according to your activities during the day.

9. You work a part-time job for which you are paid $5.80 an hour. Does the amount you are paid increase more quickly, more slowly or at the same speed as your total work hours increase? Explain your reasoning.

10. Imagine taking a trip by car and growing closer and closer to your destination. Your gas gauge is measuring less and less gas in your tank, and the distance to your destination is growing less and less. Clearly both are decreasing. Is one decreasing more rapidly?

11. The following graphs show four types of increasing change. Match each statement with one of the graphs, if possible, and tell what is changing over time.

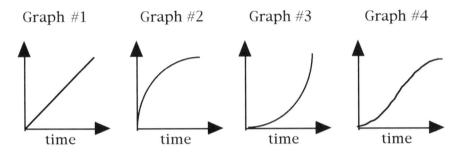

a. It seemed like there were just a few cases of AIDS, but the number grew large almost before we realized it.
b. Martha started her walk at a brisk pace, but slowed down as she got tired.
c. Many people rushed to get their tickets the first day of the show, but sales were strong all week.
d. The Johnson Company reported that their profits rose steadily over the past six months.
e. The ecoli bacteria grew quickly.
f. Mr. Means hoisted the flag to the top of the flagpole.
g. My can of pop warmed up when I left it in the warm room.
h. Mrs. Means set her cruise control and drove for several hours.

12. The following graphs show people's activity over a time of 30 seconds. Describe what each person must have been doing. Some of the graphs may not be correct. If a graph does not make sense, explain why.

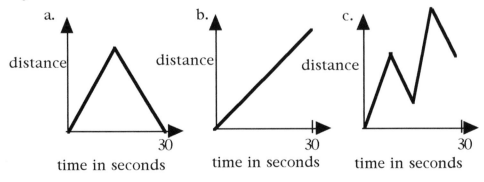

13. In the following situations, sketch a graph to show the way that the changing quantities are related. Tell which one is changing more quickly than the other.

a. How much you pay for pizza is related to the pizza's diameter.

b. Your height above or below the water's surface in a swimming pool is related to the time that has passed since you jumped off the diving board.

c. The amount of time your iced tea has stood on a table in a warm room is related to its temperature.

d. After starting with a full tank of gas, the amount of gas left in your tank is related to how far you have driven.

e. The amount of water in your bathtub is related to the number of seconds since you pulled the plug.

f. The temperature of your cappuccino is related to the time that it has been sitting on the table.

g. When you drop an egg out your bedroom window, the height of the window is related to how far the egg is from the ground.

h. A person's age and height are related.

Chapter 13
Rates

1. Do this investigation.

a. The following rectangle is divided into $\frac{1}{4}$-inch squares. Shade $\frac{2}{5}$ of the small squares in the following figure. What is the ratio of shaded to unshaded squares?

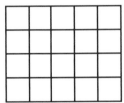

b. Reunitize the same area using a chunk consisting of two $\frac{1}{4}$-inch squares; that is, in terms of $\frac{1}{2}$-inch by $\frac{1}{4}$-inch rectangles. (Hint: You can reunitize by tracing the rectangles with a red pen in the figure above. You should trace 10 small rectangles on the figure.) What is the ratio of shaded to unshaded rectangles?

c. Reunitize the same area using a chunk consisting of 4 of the $\frac{1}{4}$-inch squares, that is, in $\frac{1}{2}$-inch squares. What is the ratio of shaded to unshaded squares?

d. Based on your drawings in a, b, and c, identify three equivalent ratios. How do you know they are equivalent?

e. Graph the ratios by putting number of shaded squares or rectangles on the vertical axis and unshaded on the horizontal axis.

f. Determine the coordinates of other points on the line.

g. Determine if these points lie on the graph: (3,7), (13, 8.67), $(\frac{3}{4}, 1\frac{1}{2})$, (6,4), (96,64).

h. What is the constant associated with this equivalence class?

i. What is the slope of the line?

j. Using the same grid, make a graph showing comparisons that may be described by a 2:1 relationship.

k. What is the constant associated with {2:1}?

l. Looking at the graphs you have drawn, can you predict where the line for {2:4} would lie?

m. How did you decide it location?

miles in $1\frac{1}{2}$ hours. What was the speed of the current?

2. Compare these rates by finding the constant associated with their equivalence classes.
a. 30 heartbeats in 15 seconds; 64 heartbeats in 30 seconds.
b. a loss of 30 pounds in 7 months; a loss of 8 pounds in 6 weeks.

3. Marcia graphed the amount of water (vertical scale) against the amount of sugar (horizontal scale) in each of 3 lemonade recipes. The line for recipe C turned out to the steepest, and the line for recipe B, the flattest.
a. Which recipe was tasted sweetest?
b. How would you interpret a horizontal line in this situation?

4. As the cold front gripped they city, the temperature dropped rapidly.
Between 4 and 5 pm, the temperature fell 10 degrees.
Between 5 and 6 pm, the temperature fell 8 degrees.
Between 6 and 7 pm, the temperature fell 6 degrees.
Between 7 and 8 pm, the temperature fell 7 degrees.
a. How much did the temperature drop between 4 pm and 6 pm?
b. What was the average rate of change between 4 pm and 6 pm?
c. What is the difference between the information given by your answer for a and for b?
d. What was the average rate of change between 6 pm and 8 pm?
e. What was the average rate of change between 4 pm and 8 pm?
f. Why are your answers for b, d, and f all different?

5. The population of the US is about 250,000,000 people and medical costs for the year were about $475,000,000,000. What does the following division tell us?
$$\$475,000,000,000 \div 250,000,000$$

6. Are these rates the same? Explain.
a. $3 per pound and 3 pounds per dollar
b. 3 meters per second and 3 seconds per meter

7. Explain how you could compute the speed of a stream by timing a wooden boat as it is carried downstream.

8. Mary, Tom, and Dennis all started from the same place at the same time, but each had a different destination. Mary drove for 3 hours. Tom drove at 75 mph. Dennis set his cruise control at 55 mph and drove for 2 hours. Which person went farthest?

9. I ran the mile in 10 minutes. How far did I run in 1 minute?

10. An empty canoe that was not tied down floated down the river, going 7 miles in $1\frac{1}{2}$ hours. What was the speed of the current?

11. A boy can bike a mile in 5 minutes and walk a mile in 20 minutes. How much time does he save if he bikes to his dad's office, 8 miles away, rather than walking?

12. The temperature fell an average of 5 degrees between the hours of 4 pm and 10 pm.
a. What was the temperature drop during those hours?
b. What was the temperature drop during the first hour, 4-5 pm?

13. Mike drove for 3 hours and traveled 110 miles. Then he got a flat and had to walk the rest of the way to his destination. He walked the last 11 miles in 2.5 hours.
a. What was his average speed on the first part of the trip?
b. What was his average speed on the second part of the trip?
c. What was his average speed for the whole journey?

14. A biker rides at a speed of 10 mph for about half an hour and then turns around and walks home on the same route, at a speed of 4 miles per hour. What is his average speed for the entire trip?

15. You are driving home from a concert with you cruise control on, and you notice that you are 10 miles from home when you have been driving for 10 minutes and 6 miles from home when you have been driving for 15 minutes.
a. How far from home was the concert?
b. How long did it take to drive home?
c. What was your speed?

16. Just for fun, we timed Mark while he was walking, running, swimming, and crawling, for 30 seconds each time. Here are his results:

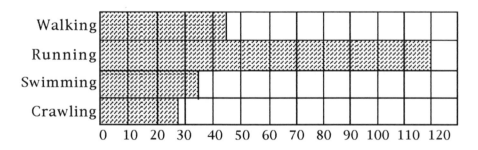

Assuming that he can keep up his pace in each activity, make a graph showing how far would he could travel in 3 minutes while moving in each of the four ways. Use graph paper and be precise. Use the graph to determine how long it would take him under each of the four conditions to travel 300 meters.

17. Carrie climbed Crow's Peak at the rate of $1\frac{1}{2}$ miles per hour and came down at the rate of $4\frac{1}{2}$ miles per hour. It took her 6 hours to travel both ways.
a. How high is the top of the peak?
b. How long did it take her to get down?

18. Jim and Ken are brothers and they are both on the track team. They frequently race each other in practice, giving Jim a bit of an advantage because he is younger and his best speed is only 3 meters per second. Ken runs 5 meters per second. This week, they ran a 150-meter race, and gave Jim a 30-meter head start. Which brother won the race? How far into the race did he pass the loser?

19. A shoe company sells 500 pairs of shoes a day if the price is $46 a pair and 430 pair a day if the price is $54 a pair. What is the rate of change of sales with respect to price?

20. A bus travels 2 miles uphill and its average speed on the way up is 25 mph. At what speed would it have to travel down the hill so that the average speed for the entire trip is 40 mph?

Chapter 14
Reasoning Proportionally

1. Does each situation involve proportional relationships, inversely proportional relationships, or neither? How can you tell?

a. The intensity of light reaching your book from a bulb depends on how far from the bulb your book is. If you are holding the book 3 meters from the bulb, the intensity is 120 units, and at 6 meters away from the bulb, it is 30 units.

b. During her first 3 months, the Carter's new baby grew an inch per month. Think how tall she will be by her first birthday!

c. Last semester, 7 people in the class of 30 students got an A in the course. This semester there are 39 students in the lecture and there will probably be 9 or 10 A students.

d. A certain kind of protozoa doubles in mass every 4 hours. In a day, its mass should become 64 times greater.

e. The more time you spend studying, the better your grades should be.

f. When the triplets mow the lawn together, they get the entire acre mowed in $1\frac{1}{4}$ hours, but if only two of the do it, it takes them just under 2 hours.

g. Earlier today, you exchanged $30 US for £20, and just now, exchanged $100 US for £66.66.

h. A subscription to my favorite magazine is priced as follows: 6 months for $15; 9 months for $22.50; 12 months for $30.

i. My telephone bill includes a flat fee of $13 plus $.09 for every local call placed.

2. Solve each of these problems using a proportion table:

a. Material costs $2.99 a meter.   How much will Ellen pay for $5\frac{3}{8}$ meters?

b. What would 5.16 pounds of grapes cost if they are priced at $1.29 per pound?

c. Find the following quotient rounded to two decimal places : 1538 ÷ 36.

Remember that to round to 2 decimal places, you must have 3 decimal places in your answer.

3. Solve each of the following problems, if possible, using any method except by solving a symbolic proportion. If a solution is not possible, state why.

a. If a puppy weighs 4.5 pounds at 3 months, how much will it weigh at 1 year?

b. If $5,000 in a savings account earns $175 interest in a year, how much would $6,525 earn in the same type of account?

c. A sugar cookie recipe calls for 2 cups of sugar and $1\frac{1}{4}$ cups of shortening. Marie has only $1\frac{1}{3}$ cups of sugar and decides to make a smaller batch. How much shortening should she use?

d. Six boys can pick 80 quarts of blueberries in day. A farmer gets an order for 350 quarts of blueberries for the next day. How many boys should he hire?

e. Pete can eat 3 large pancakes in 6 minutes. How long will it take him to eat 30 of the same size?

f. In his first 55 official times at bat a baseball player hits 3 home runs. If he expects to maintain that record and come to bat officially 460 times during the season, how many home runs can he expect to hit?

4. Analyze each situation. Use a quantity diagram to show the multiplicative relationships.

a. A subscription to my favorite magazine is priced as follows: 6 months for $18.80; 9 months for $28; 12 months for $37.

b. The area of the base of a box is 25 sq. in. The height is 4 inches. If I hold the height constant and increase the area of the base to 36 square inches, will the volume increase proportionally?

c. My telephone bill includes a flat fee of $13 plus $.09 for every local call placed during the month.

5. Six children use 1.5 tubes of toothpaste in a week. At the same rate, how many tubes of the same size will 4 children use in a month?

6. When Steve stood beside the staircase, he was 5 steps tall.

Steve and his friend Karl decided to measure their heights using bricks and the found that
Steve measured 8 bricks;
Karl measured 10 bricks.
What would Karl's height be if he stood beside the staircase?

7. John and his friends want to decorate some large sugar cookies by using 3 jellybeans (for the eyes and nose) and 5 M&M's[®](for the mouth) to make a happy face on each cookie.
a. John's mother gave them 42 jelly beans and 60 M&M's.[®] How many cookies can the children decorate?
b. The next time she made cookies, John's mother sent the children to the store to get one bag of each type of candy. The drug store sells jellybeans in bags of 45 and 72. M&Ms[®]come in bags of 60 and 100. John knows that after he and his friends decorate as many cookies as possible, his mother will give them the extra candy to eat. Which two bags should he buy in order to have the most pieces of candy left to eat?

8. Two statues, bored from standing in the same position for so long, struck up a conversation.
Statue A said, "It would be difficult to move my weight together with that of the base I stand on."
B: "My base and I weigh as much."
A: "But I alone weight twice as much as your base."
B: "I alone weigh three times the weight of your base."
How do the weights of the statues compare to each other?

9. For each situation,
i.   determine whether there is a proportional relationship or an inversely proportional relationship;
ii. write an equation relating the two variables

a. If a certain lever is 30 inches long, a force of 63 pounds is required to move an object. If a similar lever is 10 inches, long, a force of 189 pounds is required to move the object.

b. If you recycle 23 pounds of aluminum, you are paid $9.20, and if you recycle 50 pounds, you are paid $20.

c. Under 46 psi pressure, a certain gas has a volume of 360 cu. ft., while 60 psi of pressure compresses the volume of the gas to 276 cu. ft.

10. At the grocery store the price of a pint of milk is $.64. The price of a quart (2 pints) is $1.19. Can you predict the price of a gallon (4 quarts)?

Chapter 15
Applications: Similarity and Percents

1. The following rectangles are similar. Find the missing measurement on the smaller rectangle by scaling down.

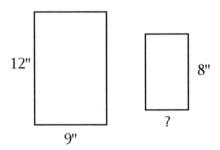

2. If two rectangles were congruent (that is, they have the same size and shape), what would be the relationship between their widths?

3. On the following grid, each square is 1 unit by 1 unit. On a piece of graph paper, draw a rectangle of the same shape that will fit on the grid, but whose dimensions are not whole numbers. How did you decide how long and how wide your rectangle should be?

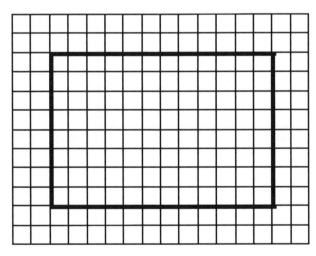

4. You will need to make copies of these rectangles and cut them out. Use them to answer the following questions.
A rectangle is in R's family if it has the same shape as R.
a. Which rectangle(s) belong in R's family?
b. What is the ratio of sides in the R family?

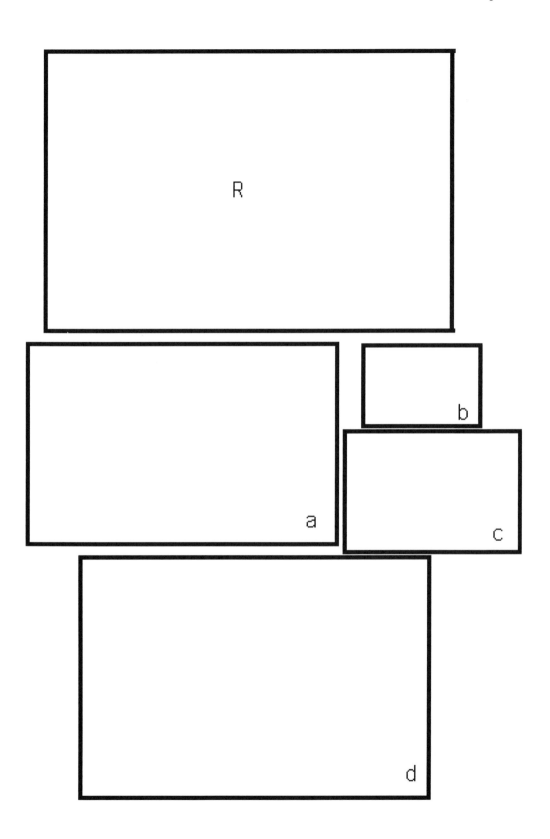

5. These letters are the same shape, but a different size. How long is the curve marked x?

6. a. What is the scale factor when a 2" square is enlarged to become a 6" square?
b. By what factor is its area enlarged?

7. Answer each question by reasoning:
a. 15% of 80 = _____
b. 15 = _____% of 50
c. 20% of 70 = _____
d. 35% of _____ = 21
e. 27 is 45% of _____

8. Marvin wants to buy his mother a book for her birthday. It standardly sells for $15.95, but during a special promotion, every book store he knew had a sale! Where should he buy it? At store A, the book is 5% off; at B, it is $.50 off; at C, it is $.50 off on the dollar; at D, it is $\frac{1}{5}$ off; and at E, it is 50% off.

9. Mike sold his car to Kathy at a 10% loss. Later, she sold it back to him at a 10% gain. How does Mike do in the end? What percent profit or loss did he realize?

10. Use a ratio table to solve the each of the following problems:
a. 23 is 15% of ?
b. 42 is 36% of ?
c. 26 is ___% of 74 (To two decimal places.)

11. In your favorite department at Boss Store, you find a clearance rack that is marked "35% Off Already Discounted Prices." The skirt you want to buy was originally $49.99 and the ticket now says $39.99. How much will you pay, and what percent discount are you actually getting?

Part III
Discussion of Supplementary Activities

Chapter 2
Relative and Absolute Thinking

1. B contains 5 more stars than box A, and it contains $2\frac{2}{3}$ times the number of stars in box A. Box A contains $\frac{3}{8}$ times the number of stars in box B. Another way to say it is that set A is $\frac{3}{8}$ of set B. If a group is defined as a set of 2 stars, the A contains $1\frac{1}{2}$ groups and B contains 4 groups.

2. You cannot tell which pool has the greater capacity if you know only the ground-level dimensions of the pools. The capacity depends on the area you can see (length x width of the pool) as well as on the depth. So, for example, if the depth of the first pool were 2 feet and the depth of the second pool were 14 feet, the capacity of the second pool would be greater. If the depth of the first pool were 6 feet and the depth of the second pool were 35 feet, the capacity of the first pool would be 480 cubic feet, while the capacity of the second would be only 240 cubic feet.

3. $10 off the dress is a 22% savings ($\frac{\$10}{\$44.99}$), whereas $10 off the blouse represents a more substantial discount ($\frac{\$10}{\$26.99}$) of 37%.

4. How orangy a drink will taste depends on the amount of orange mix as compared to the amount of water in the drink. One can of orange juice in a quart of water will taste more orangy than a can of orange juice dissolved in a half gallon of water.

5. There are many characteristics that are measured as a comparison of two quantities. A few examples are given here. Gas consumption in your car cannot be measured merely by counting how many gallons of gas your car used. Knowing a person's weight cannot tell you if the person is overweight. To determine whether a light will be strong enough for reading, it is not enough to know the bulb's wattage. All of these characteristics require a comparison of quantities.

6. A grasshopper is much smaller than a human. Yet, pound for pound, it can jump much higher than a human can jump. Our mass is probably more than 1,000 times greater than that of a grasshopper, but we cannot jump 1,000 times as high as it can.

7.   In a little more than 45 years, the population of Manhattan has grown over 126% but the area has grown much faster than the population. The area in 1950 was just a little over 1583 acres. If the ratio of people to acres were the same now as in 1950, there would be about 3,583 acres. But 5 people per acre means that there are now 8,600 acres, so the area has increased by about 443%. The area of the city has been expanding much more rapidly than the population. (This, in turn, means that people are enjoying the luxury of lots of space around them, but taxpayers are paying a much larger percentage of the cost of providing roads and services over such a large area.)

8. Considering only absolute numbers of females, the Game Room has more females. However, if you look at the number of females in each place as compared to the total number of customers in each,   they had equal proportions of females. The Dew Drop had 12 females out of 19 customers or $\frac{12}{19}$ = 63% females and the Game Room had 24 females out of 38 customers or $\frac{24}{38}$ = 63% females.

9. This investigation is a demonstration that addition does not always make larger. Enlarging is a multiplicative process. Adding to the coordinates of the rectangle you started with merely moved it (translated it) in the coordinate plane. Repeatedly adding to the coordinates of the original figure will continue to move it in the plane, so neither is multiplication repeated addition!

Chapter 3
Fractions and Rational Numbers

1.   This   problem may be solved in two ways.   As a multiplication problem: If $\frac{2}{3}$ liter costs \$1.89, then a full liter, which is $1\frac{1}{2}$ times as much as $\frac{2}{3}$ liter, must cost $\frac{3}{2}$ (\$1.89) or \$2.84.   As a division followed by a multiplication: Divide \$1.89 by 2 to get the cost of $\frac{1}{3}$ liter.   Dividing by 2 is the same as multiplying by $\frac{1}{2}$, so $\frac{1}{2}$ (\$1.89) = \$.945 or $94\frac{1}{2}$ cents.   Next, multiply by 3 to get the price of a full liter.   3(\$.945) = \$2.84.   But multiplying by $\frac{1}{2}$ and then multiplying by 3 is the same as multiplying by $\frac{3}{2}$.

2. If each step were exactly 1 meter in length, it would take 10 steps to cover a distance of 10 meters. Because each step measures less than 1 meter, it will take more than 10 steps to cover a distance of 10 meters. We can reinterpret the questions in this way: Each step measures .75 m. How many of these steps can we measure out of a distance of 10 m? This is a division problem.   10m ÷ .75m = 13 steps and another step that measures $\frac{1}{3}$ m.

3. This problem calls for multiplication. You know the price per pound. If you were buying 3 pounds, you would multiply by 3. When you are buying a fraction of a pound, you multiply by the fraction of a pound. $\frac{\$4.29}{1 \text{pound}} \cdot \frac{.94 \text{ pounds}}{1} = \$4.03$.

4. \$1.84 per £ is $\frac{\$1.84}{1£}$. Another way to say \$1.84 per 1£ is 1£ per \$1.84. For every \$1.84, you can get 1£. So we want to know how many times we can take \$1.84 out of \$500. This is a division problem. \$500 ÷ \$1.84 = 271.74 £ or 271 £ 74 pence (pennies).

5.   This problem can be solved by multiplication or by multiplication followed by division (but multiplication followed by division amounts to a fraction multiplication).

$$\frac{240 \text{ cars}}{3 \text{ cartons}} \div \frac{10 \text{ boxes}}{1 \text{ carton}} = \frac{240 \text{ cars}}{3 \text{ cartons}} \cdot \frac{1 \text{ carton}}{10 \text{ boxes}} = \frac{240 \text{ cars}}{30 \text{ boxes}} = \frac{8 \text{ cars}}{1 \text{ box}}.$$

6. A 3-unit would be something like 3 jawbreakers in a package or 3 cupcakes in a package. The first operation below shows the result of taking $\frac{1}{3}$ of the package or $\frac{1}{3}$ of the 3-unit. The result is $\frac{1}{3}$ of the package. In the second operation, if each item represents $\frac{1}{3}$ of a package, then 3 of those one-third units is three items, which, in turn, is equivalent to a whole package or 1 unit.

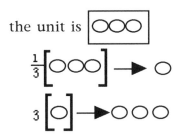

7. A 12-unit would be something like a dozen eggs—12 items grouped into one package. A 3-unit is one package containing 3 items. Although a 12-unit and four 3-units contain the same number of eggs, they are named by different fractions. One 12-unit is called 1 or 1 unit. Four 3-units has the name 4 or 4 units.

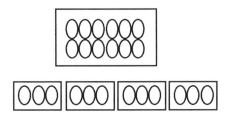

Chapter 4
Units and Unitizing

1. a. If $1\frac{2}{3} = \frac{5}{3}$ is 10 strips, then $\frac{1}{3}$ is 2 strips, so $\frac{3}{3} = 1$ is 6 strips.

b. Because 5 orks = 15 squares, 1 ork = 3 squares and $\frac{1}{3}$ ork = 1 square. $1\frac{2}{3} = \frac{5}{3}$ orks must be 5 squares.

c. If $\frac{1}{5}$ is 4 stars, then $\frac{5}{5} = 1$ is 20 stars. $\frac{1}{4}$ is 5 stars and $\frac{3}{4}$ is 15 stars.

d. If 9 triangles $= \frac{3}{7}$, then 3 triangles $= \frac{1}{7}$. So $\frac{5}{7}$ must be 15 triangles.

e. If $\frac{1}{2}$ is 2 circles, then $\frac{2}{2} = 1$ must be 4 circles. $\frac{8}{8}$ is 4 circles and $\frac{1}{8}$ is $\frac{1}{2}$ circle, so $\frac{3}{8}$ is $1\frac{1}{2}$ circles.

2. For the child who is just beginning to study fractions with part—whole comparisons, this picture is confusing in more than one respect. First of all, it uses two different units. The first two fractions are shaded on a unit consisting of 2 squares, but the third fraction is shaded on a unit twice the size of the first unit. For the child who knows that $\frac{1}{2}$ and $\frac{2}{4}$ are equivalent fractions, the picture is terribly confusing because equivalent fractions should cover the same area (and hence look the same) on the same area model. However, the addition is not correct and so it makes little sense to try to picture it anyway.

We would not want to use this picture with children whose only interpretation of fractions was the part—whole comparison.
However, as we have already pointed out, the same fraction notation may be used to convey many different meanings. The fractions in this picture may be interpreted as ratios; ratio addition is different from addition with part—whole comparisons. If we interpret the first two pictures as "1 out of 2" then 1 out of 2 and another 1 out of 2 gives 2 out of 4. You can think about this in a baseball context. If you hit 1 ball out of 2 and later in the practice hit 1 ball out of 2, then for the day, you hit 2 out of 4 balls. But even if we limit the discussion to ratio situations, we still must take great care to make sure that pictures correspond with interpretations. For example, we could write 1: 2 or $\frac{1}{2}$ meaning a ratio of 1 shaded square to 2 nonshaded squares. For this interpretation, the pictures do not work.

3. Tim's unit or total amount of money could have been different from Pete's unit or total amount of money. For example, Tim could have $200 and Pete could have $50. If Tim spent $\frac{1}{4}$ of his money, he would spend $50, and if Pete spent $\frac{1}{2}$ of his money, he would spend $25. So it is possible that Tim spend more money in actual dollars, but that the amount he spent is relatively less than the amount Pete spent, that is, less when you compare what each person spent to the total amount of money he had.

4. When you made your drawing of the gum, did you draw packs or individual pieces? Or did you draw a pack with the 5 pieces marked on it? The point is that because the gum was presented as a composite unit, that is, it was a single package with 5 sticks inside, there were different ways in which you could have drawn the 2 full packs. To represent the $\frac{3}{5}$ of a pack, you had to unitize 1(5-pack) as 5(1-units). On the other hand, the candies are given as single pieces and if any grouping occurs it is your own. You do not have to start with some imposed unit. Second, the individual sticks of gum are items that can be cut into equal-sized pieces, but we do not typically try to cut hard candies into pieces. This difference affects the usefulness of each type of item for showing various fractional parts. For example, it was easy to show $2\frac{1}{4}$ times the number of hard candies, but you would not ask children to show $2\frac{3}{5}$ times that number. With the gum, you could represent $2\frac{1}{4}$ packs by splitting pieces. As adults, we can underestimate the effects of these differences on children's thinking. Which sorts of items you ask children to use and the numbers you give them can dramatically affect difficulty.

5. $1\frac{1}{2}$ recs = 3 blocks = $4\frac{1}{2}$ railroad tracks = 9 longs = 18 sticks = 36 mini-longs = 108 mini-blocks = 54 mini-sticks = 18 mini-recs.

6. Many questions are possible. Here are a few. Questions refer to Rec 3.

1 rec = _____ blocks   Ans. $\frac{2}{3}$ block

1 rec = _____ rec1   Ans. $\frac{1}{3}$ rec1

1 rec = _____ rec2   Ans. $\frac{3}{7}$

7. a. 3 weeks = 21 days = $\frac{3}{4}$ month

b. $\$.05 = \frac{1}{2}$ dime $= \frac{1}{20}$ dollar

c. $16 \left(\frac{1}{2}\text{-pints}\right) = 4$ quarts $= 1$ gallon

d. $1\frac{1}{2}$ dozen $= 18$ singles $= 3\left(\frac{1}{2}\text{-dozen}\right)$

e. $26\left(\frac{1}{4}\text{-miles}\right) = 13\left(\frac{1}{2}\text{-miles}\right) = 6\frac{1}{2}$ miles

f. 3 inches $= \frac{1}{4}$ foot $= \frac{1}{12}$ yard

g. $5(5\text{-packs}) = 25$ sticks $= 1\frac{8}{17}(17\text{-packs})$

h. 17 pairs $= 34$ singles $= 1\frac{7}{10}(10\text{-packs})$

i. $3(8\text{-packs}) = 1(24\text{-pack}) = 2(12\text{-packs})$

Chapter 5
Part-Whole Comparisons

1. We do not need to know the exact numbers of animals to answer the question. Whatever the number of cats is, the number of dogs is $\frac{5}{3}$ the number of cats. The number of cats is the unit. Let a rectangle represent the number of cats and divide it into thirds. Take a piece the size of $\frac{1}{3}$ and duplicate it 5 times to represent $\frac{5}{3}$, the number of dogs.

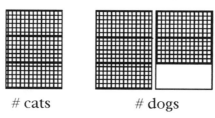

cats   # dogs

The town of Rosedale has fewer cats. The number of dogs is $1\frac{2}{3}$ times the number of cats.

2. $\dfrac{4 \text{ couples}}{12 \text{ people}} = \dfrac{2 \text{ quads}}{3 \text{ quads}}$

So 4 couples take up $\frac{2}{3}$ of a row.

No matter how you unitize, there are always the same number of people and the same number of seats. They are merely grouped differently—first in pairs, then as singles, then in 4-groups. So you get $\frac{4}{6}$ of a row when you unitize in pairs, $\frac{8}{12}$ of a row when you unitize as individuals, and $\frac{2}{3}$ when you unitize as quads, but they are equivalent.

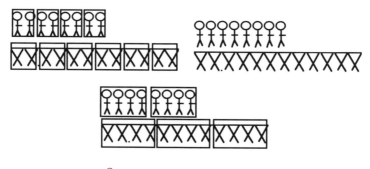

3. $\dfrac{10 \text{ cents}}{100 \text{ cents}} = \dfrac{1 \text{ dime}}{10 \text{ dimes}} = \dfrac{\frac{2}{5} \text{ quarter}}{4 \text{ quarters}} = \dfrac{2 \text{ nickels}}{20 \text{ nickels}}$

4. A cube has 6 faces, all having the same area. One face must be $\frac{1}{6}$ of the total surface area.

5. $\frac{2^2}{2^5} = \frac{1}{2^3} = \frac{1}{8}$

6. There are 20 diamonds. That's 5 (4-packs). You need 3(4-packs) or 12 diamonds.

7. Think of the 20 diamonds as 10 (2-packs). You need 7 (2-packs) or 14 diamonds.

8. In relation to the set of bugs, $\frac{5}{6}$ means $\frac{5 \text{ groups of } 4}{6 \text{ groups of } 4} = 20$ bugs.
$\frac{11}{12}$ means $\frac{11 \text{ pair}}{12 \text{ pair}} = 22$ bugs.
$\frac{7}{8}$ means $\frac{7 \text{ groups of } 3}{8 \text{ groups of } 3} = 21$ bugs.

$\frac{5}{6}$ is the smallest.

Chapter 6
Partitioning and Quotients

1. Halves of the same candy bar cannot be of different sizes or they should not be called halves. Children often refer to "his half" and "my half" without knowing the meaning of the word "half" and when they really mean two pieces. Most likely, the candy bar was cut into pieces, but they were not of the same size. The child who was upset got the smaller of the two pieces.

2. Yes. One solution would look like this:

3. Yes. Stacy's solution is correct. Both children got half a cookie and one had three pieces and the other, two pieces.

4. Here are three possible partitions.

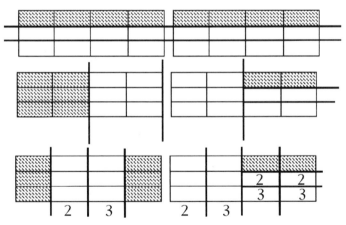

The resulting shares are $\frac{4}{12} + \frac{4}{12}$, $\frac{6}{12} + \frac{2}{12}$, and $\frac{3}{12} + \frac{3}{12} + \frac{2}{12}$.

$\frac{3}{12} + \frac{3}{12} = \frac{6}{12}$.

5. Each picture shows fourths. Each unit is partitioned into four equal shares. Their sizes and orientations relative to each other are not important.

6. One share will be $\frac{2}{3}$ of a candy bar, or $\frac{1}{3}$ of the unit.

7. One share will be $\frac{6}{8}$ or $\frac{3}{4}$ of a cheese pizza and $\frac{4}{8}$ or $\frac{1}{2}$ of a mushroom pizza. $\frac{6}{8} + \frac{4}{8}$ describes the portions of each type of pizza in a share, but $\frac{6}{8} + \frac{4}{8} = \frac{12}{8}$ does not describe one share because there are two different units in this problem. Nevertheless, each person gets $\frac{1}{8}$ of the pizza.

8. Each girl will get 1 whole pepperoni pizza and $1\frac{1}{3}$ cheese pizzas. If she then shares her portion with her sister, each girl will eat $\frac{1}{2}$ pepperoni pizza and $\frac{2}{3}$ of a cheese pizza, which is $\frac{1}{6}$ of the total amount of pizza.

9. The part—whole question asked in partitioning problem becomes much more difficult to answer in a quotitive division problem that has a fractional answer. In the rope problem, there are 9 pieces of rope, but each is not $\frac{1}{9}$ of the whole rope because there is a small piece left over.

10. Here is one picture that shows that 4 people could be served and there would be some left over.

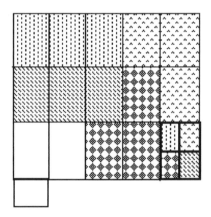

What part of a serving is the extra part of the package? Unitize in quarter ounces.

$$\frac{2\frac{1}{2} \text{ ounces}}{3\frac{1}{4} \text{ ounces}} = \frac{10 \ (\frac{1}{4}\text{-ounces})}{13 \ (\frac{1}{4}\text{-ounces})}.$$

Therefore, the box contains $4\frac{10}{13}$ servings.

11. Here is one possibility:

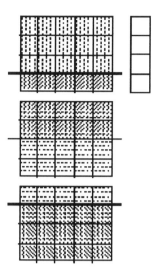

There are 4 and $\dfrac{\frac{1}{5}\text{ mile}}{\frac{3}{4}\text{-mile}}$ stretches. Unitize in $\dfrac{1}{20}$-miles.

$$\frac{\frac{1}{5}\text{ mile}}{\frac{3}{4}\text{-mile}} = \frac{4\ (\frac{1}{20}\text{-miles})}{15\ (\frac{1}{20}\text{-miles})}.$$

Therefore, the team needs 5 runners.. The first four will do a $\dfrac{3}{4}$-mile stretch and the last one will do only $\dfrac{4}{15}$ stretch.

12. $\dfrac{3\frac{1}{4}\text{ ounces}}{15\frac{1}{2}\text{ ounces}} = \dfrac{13(\frac{1}{4}\text{-ounces})}{62(\frac{1}{4}\text{-ounces})}$, so one serving is $\dfrac{13}{62}$ of a package. Note that 4 of these servings do not make a total package, but only $\dfrac{52}{62}$ package. This is because there is a partial serving, $\dfrac{10}{13}$ serving, that consists of $2\frac{1}{2}$ ounces or $\dfrac{5}{31}$ package.

Chapter 7
Rational Numbers as Operators

1. Multiplying by $\frac{3}{2}$, or enlarging to $1\frac{1}{2}$ its original size.

2. Multiplying by $\frac{4}{5}$, or reducing to $\frac{4}{5}$ of its original size.

3. $\frac{1}{4}$ of the starting quantity is increased to 7 times its size. In symbols, this is $7(\frac{1}{4}(8)) = 14$. The composite operation is multiplication by $\frac{7}{4}$ and $\frac{7}{4}(8) = 14$.

4. Both exchangers give the same output for the same input.

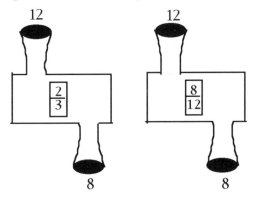

Other exchange machines that would yield the same results are a 4-for-6 machine, a 16-for-24 machine, and a 24-for-36 machine.

5.

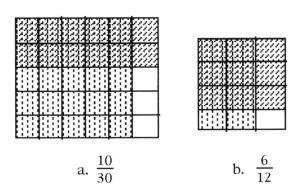

a. $\frac{10}{30}$ b. $\frac{6}{12}$

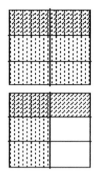

c. $\frac{3}{6}$

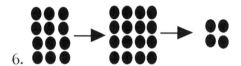

6.

7. The first operator exchanges 5 for 10 , so it is a $\frac{5}{10}$ or $\frac{1}{2}$ operator.

The second exchanges 2 for 10, so it is a $\frac{2}{10}$ or $\frac{1}{5}$ operator. $\frac{1}{2}$ must be larger because the second operator reduced the size by more than half.

8.

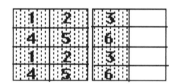   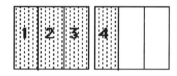

a. 2   b. $\frac{4}{6}$

9. The 12 males are $\frac{3}{4}$ of $\frac{2}{3}$ the number of people or $\frac{1}{2}$ the number of people, so the number of people is 24. The number of female children is $\frac{1}{4}(\frac{1}{3}(24))$ or 2.

1/3	1/4	1/12
2/3	1/2	1/6

3/4   1/4

10. $\frac{1}{3} = \frac{4}{12}$ and $\frac{1}{4} = \frac{3}{12}$. $\frac{1}{3} > \frac{1}{4}$.

11. $\frac{3}{8}=\frac{9}{24}$ and $\frac{1}{6}=\frac{4}{24}$

12.

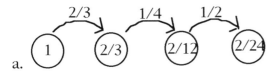

a.

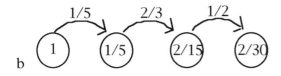

b

Chapter 8
Rational Numbers as Measures

1. By successively partitioning until you have thirty-seconds, you can see that you have about $\frac{23}{32}$ of an hour, or 43 minutes. (You should get something close to .72.)

2. By partitioning the quarter-hour interval into 4 equal pieces, you get sixteenths of an hour. Your meter has $\frac{1}{16}$ hr. on it and you need $\frac{8}{16}$ of an hour, so you must pay for $\frac{7}{16}$ of an hour or $26\frac{1}{4}$ minutes. You should deposit 1 quarter and 1 dime.

3. a. If the given interval is $\frac{5}{9}$, then partition it into 5 equal pieces, each of which is $\frac{1}{9}$. Add another interval that is as long as 4 of those interval to get a unit interval.

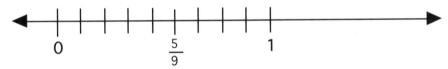

b. Successively partition the given interval until you have 9 equal subintervals. Because 9 subintervals = $\frac{9}{4}$, 1 subinterval must be $\frac{1}{4}$, and the unit interval must be 4 subintervals.

c. Partition the given interval into 10 subintervals. Then each is $\frac{1}{17}$. By adding an interval the length of 7 of them, you get the unit interval.

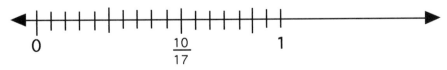

4. You get 38 minutes on the meter, which is $\frac{38}{60}$ or $\frac{19}{30}$ of an hour. Successively partition the hour until you have thirtieths (sixths then

fifths). The first half hour is $\frac{15}{30}$ and four subintervals past the half hour (moving counterclockwise) is $\frac{19}{30}$. (Your answer may be close.)

5. a. Divide the interval (A,B) into 2 equal parts. Then each of those is $\frac{1}{3}$. Add an interval of length $\frac{1}{3}$ to the right of B and then the interval from A to that point is the unit interval ($\frac{3}{3}$). Partition the unit interval into 4 equal parts and add one of those parts to the right of 1. Label the new point X. (A,X) measures $1\frac{1}{4}$ unit intervals.

b. Successively partition the interval (C,D) until you have sixteen subunits. Fifteen of them constitute 1 unit interval. Partition each of the $\frac{1}{15}$-units into 2 parts so that you have thirtieths. 7 of those subintervals to the right of C is $\frac{7}{30}$.

c. Partition (E,F) into 7 equal parts. 3 of them constitute the unit interval. Add $\frac{2}{3}$ of the unit to the right of F and then you have 3 units. Partition the unit interval again so that you have ninths. Add an interval the length of $\frac{5}{9}$ to the right of 3 and you have $3\frac{5}{9}$ unit intervals.

d. Successively partition (G,H) until you have 11 subintervals. Each is $\frac{1}{15}$. Add an interval of the length $\frac{4}{15}$ to the right of H and then you have a unit interval. Notice that $\frac{1}{5}=\frac{3}{15}$ and $\frac{3}{5}=\frac{9}{15}$. Add an interval of length $\frac{9}{15}$ to the right of F and then you have $1\frac{3}{5}$.

6. a. If you partition the interval between 1 hour and $1\frac{1}{2}$ hours into three equal parts, then the $\frac{1}{2}$ hour is partitioned into $\frac{1}{6}$-hour intervals. Then the meter says that you need only $\frac{1}{6}$ hour or 10 minutes more time to have the desired $1\frac{1}{2}$ hour time limit. You should deposit 1 dime and 1 nickel.

b. Successively partition the interval between $\frac{1}{2}$ hour and 1 hour until there are 8 subintervals, then each subinterval is $\frac{1}{8}$ of $\frac{1}{2}$ or $\frac{1}{16}$ of an hour. This means that your friend has $\frac{8}{16} + \frac{1}{16}$ or $\frac{9}{16}$ hr. left on the meter. 1 hour would be $\frac{16}{16}$ and $1\frac{1}{2}$ hours would be $\frac{24}{16}$. He needs to pay for $\frac{24}{16} - \frac{9}{16} = \frac{15}{16}$ hr. or $56\frac{1}{4}$ minutes. He should deposit 3 quarters. 2 quarters, 2 dimes and 1 nickel would work, but for the same amount of money, he could get more time by using 3 quarters.

7. a. Partition the interval between $\frac{3}{8}$ and $\frac{4}{8}$ into five equal subintervals, and then the given fractions are renamed as $\frac{15}{40}$ and $\frac{20}{40}$, and $\frac{16}{40}, \frac{17}{40}, \frac{18}{40}$, and $\frac{19}{40}$ lie between them.

b. Partition the unit interval until you have sixth-fifths and then $\frac{3}{13}$ is renamed as $\frac{15}{65}$ and you have a point corresponding to $\frac{17}{65}$. If you partition each interval into three equal subintervals, then $\frac{15}{65}$ is renamed as $\frac{45}{195}$ and $\frac{17}{65}$ is renamed as $\frac{51}{195}$, and you can easily name 5 points between them: $\frac{46}{195}, \frac{47}{195}, \frac{48}{195}, \frac{49}{195}$, and $\frac{50}{195}$.

Chapter 9
Quantitative Relationships:
Visual and Verbal

1. a. The critical relationship to be explored in this question is that of the diameter (or radius) of the wheel to the circumference. The larger the radius, the greater the distance the wheel covers in one full turn. (↑ ↑) This is not as obvious to children as it may seem to you!
b. When the distance covered is the same for both wheels, the larger wheel can cover it in fewer turns; the smaller wheel will need to make more revolutions. The larger the wheel, the fewer the turns it need to make to cover some distance. (↑ ↓) The smaller the wheel, the more turns it will make in covering the same distance. (↓ ↑).

2. The tunnel questions can be difficult even for some middle school children. You would be surprised at the number who cannot answer this questions with conviction. The relationship to be explored here is that of distance and apparent size. The exit of the tunnel looks smaller because it is farther away from us. The farther away an object is, the smaller it appears. (↑ ↓)

3. You would clearly want to join Jenny's group because she has more cookies to share among the same number of people. The more cookies to share with same number of people, the more each person will get. (↑ ↑).

4. The building is not quite four times as tall as Joe. Because Joe is 5 feet tall, the building must be about 18 feet tall.

5. Check your accuracy by measuring.

6. If the pies are priced at the same rate as the packages we can see, then the unmarked package should cost $6. The more stacks per package, the higher the price. (↑ ↑). In fact, the price is the number of stacks times $6.

7. $4, 4, 4, 4\frac{1}{2}$

8. a. more
b. less
c. less
d. cannot tell
e. cannot tell
f. more
g. more
h. less

9. a. Light green is half of dark green, but purple is not half of orange. Alternatively, dark green covers $\frac{2}{3}$ of blue, but light green covers $\frac{3}{4}$ of purple. Remove the purple, and place a red on top of light green.

b. Brown covers $\frac{4}{5}$ of orange, but red covers half of purple. Alternately, red is $\frac{1}{4}$ of brown, but purple is not $\frac{1}{4}$ of orange. Remove the red, and put purple on top of yellow.

c. Light green covers $\frac{1}{3}$ of blue, but white covers half of red. Alternately, white is $\frac{1}{3}$ of light green, but red is not $\frac{1}{3}$ of blue. Replace red with light green.

10.

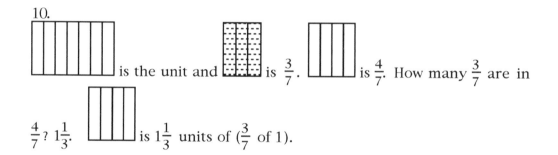

is the unit and ⬚ is $\frac{3}{7}$. ⬚ is $\frac{4}{7}$. How many $\frac{3}{7}$ are in $\frac{4}{7}$? $1\frac{1}{3}$. ⬚ is $1\frac{1}{3}$ units of ($\frac{3}{7}$ of 1).

Chapter 10
Reasoning With Fractions

1. Partitioning into eighths in one direction and sevenths the other direction divided the unit into 56ths. $\frac{3}{8} = \frac{21}{56}$ and $\frac{2}{7} = \frac{16}{56}$.

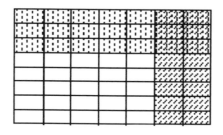

2.

a. CRP $\frac{8}{19} < \frac{1}{2}$ and $\frac{9}{17} > \frac{1}{2}$, so $\frac{8}{19} < \frac{9}{17}$.

b. SNP   Both mixed numbers are between 2 and 3 units. Comparing their fractional parts, we see that numerators are the same, so the larger fraction will have the smaller denominator. $\frac{7}{3} = 2\frac{1}{3}$ and $\frac{9}{4} = 2\frac{1}{4}$. Therefore, $\frac{7}{3} > \frac{9}{4}$.

c. CRP $\frac{7}{15} < \frac{1}{2}$ and $\frac{9}{14} > \frac{1}{2}$, so $\frac{7}{15} < \frac{9}{14}$.

3. a. $\frac{1}{14} = \frac{1\frac{1}{14}}{15}$. Choose numerators greater than 1 and less than $1\frac{1}{14}$, say, $1\frac{1}{15}$, $1\frac{1}{16}$, and $1\frac{1}{17}$. Then $\frac{1\frac{1}{15}}{15} = \frac{16}{225}$, $\frac{1\frac{1}{16}}{15} = \frac{17}{240}$, and $\frac{1\frac{1}{17}}{15} = \frac{18}{255}$ are between the given fractions.

b. $3 = \frac{15}{5}$, so choose numerators that are between 14 and 15, say $14\frac{1}{3}$, $14\frac{1}{4}$, and $14\frac{1}{5}$. Then $\frac{14\frac{1}{3}}{5} = \frac{43}{15}$, $\frac{14\frac{1}{4}}{5} = \frac{57}{20}$, and $\frac{14\frac{1}{5}}{5} = \frac{71}{25}$ are between the given fractions.

4. A medium and a large bucket hold 8 liters. A small and a large hold $6\frac{1}{4}$ liters. Together, these two facts tell us that 3 large buckets hold $14\frac{1}{4}$ liters, so 1 large bucket holds $4\frac{3}{4}$ liters. Because a medium and a large hold 8 liters, a medium bucket holds $3\frac{1}{4}$ liters. Because a small and a large hold $6\frac{1}{4}$ liters, a small bucket must hold $1\frac{1}{2}$ liters.

5. Three medium buckets hold the same amount as 5 small buckets, so 1 medium holds the same amount as $1\frac{2}{3}$ small buckets. Because 3 large hold the same as 4 medium and 2 small, 3 large hold the same as 7 small and 1 medium or $8\frac{2}{3}$ small buckets. 1 large bucket holds $2\frac{8}{9}$ small and 2 large hold $5\frac{7}{9}$ small. Therefore 2 large hold more than 3 medium.

6. $\frac{12}{25}$ is close to $\frac{1}{2}$. $\frac{1}{2}=\frac{12\frac{1}{2}}{25}$, so $\frac{12\frac{1}{4}}{25}=\frac{49}{100}$ is even closer to $\frac{1}{2}$ than $\frac{12}{25}$ is.

7. Three girls get 2 pizzas. If you match 2 pizzas to 3 boys, then you have 1 pizza left for 1 boy. After he takes a share as large as the other boys had (quotient: $\frac{2}{3}$ of a pizza), there is an extra $\frac{1}{3}$ pizza. This means that the boys have more pizza.

8. If $\frac{2}{9}$ of the class is girls, then $\frac{7}{9}$ of the class is boys. There are clearly more boys—$3\frac{1}{2}$ times as many boys as girls.

9. If b = the number of boys and g = the number of girls, then b = 2g.

10. There is more juice. If j is the amount of juice and w is the amount of water, then $j = \frac{4}{3}w$.

11. Ted is taller. If Jim's height is J and Ted's height is T, then $J = \frac{2}{3}T$.

12. A full liter will cost more than $\frac{2}{3}$ liter. If $\frac{2}{3}$ liter cost $3, then $\frac{1}{3}$ liter costs $1.50, and 1 liter costs $4.50.

13.   The largest fraction of the population that can speak all three languages is the smallest fraction that speaks one of the languages. Certainly an upper bound on the part of the population speaking all three languages would be $\frac{7}{12}$ because $\frac{7}{12}$ is the largest part that speaks French. A lower bound would be 0 because if $\frac{1}{3}$ do not speak German, $\frac{5}{12}$ do not speak French, and $\frac{1}{4}$ do not speak English, then $\frac{12}{12}$ do not speak all 3 languages. Another way to check the lower bound is to put numbers into a Venn diagram. We want to see if the intersection of all 3 sets can be 0 while maintaining $\frac{8}{12}$ in the German circle, $\frac{7}{12}$ in the French circle, and $\frac{9}{12}$ in the English circle, with all three fractions adding to $\frac{12}{12} = 1$. There are many ways in which this can be done. Two possibilities are shown here.

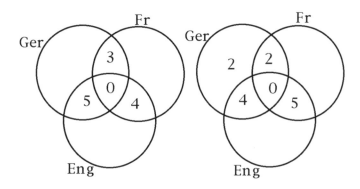

7 is the upper bound for the largest number of people who speak all three languages. By checking 7 and then 6, we find that the largest number that can be placed in the common intersection is 6. Several arrangements are possible when 6 people speak all three languages.

14. a. $1\frac{1}{10}$ is a little over 1 and $\frac{7}{8}$ is a little under 1. The sum is approximately 2.

b. $\frac{12}{13}$ is almost 1 and $\frac{3}{7}$ is about $\frac{1}{2}$. The difference is approximately $\frac{1}{2}$.

c. This product says to take a little more than half of a little more than $1\frac{1}{2}$. Your answer should be greater than $\frac{3}{4}$ and less than 1.

d. Your point should be $\frac{1}{3}$ of the way between 0 and $\frac{1}{8}$.

e. Dividing by $\frac{1}{2}$ gives you twice as much. The answer is $2\frac{1}{2}$.

Chapter 11
Ratios

1. a. If the diet drink has $\frac{2}{3}$ fewer calories, then it has $\frac{1}{3}$ the number of calories in regular drink. The ratio of calories in diet to calories in regular is 1:3.
b. The ratio of calories in Spritzer to the calories in Splash is 2:3.
c. The nationally-known brand is $1\frac{1}{2}$ times as expensive as the store brand, so the ratio of the cost of the national brand to the store brand is 3:2.
d. The ratio of crooks to honest people is 2:300.

2. 3 players got 2 pizzas; 6 players got 4 pizzas; 9 players got 6. 14 pizzas would have served 21 players. Because everyone was supposed to get the same amount, 15 pizzas would have served 22 players.

3. 18 pizzas for 24 people is equivalent to 9 pizzas for 12 people. 9 pizzas for 12 people is equivalent to 6 pizzas for 8 people and 3 pizzas for 4 people. On the other hand, 9 pizzas for 12 people is also equivalent to $4\frac{1}{2}$ pizzas for 6 people and another $4\frac{1}{2}$ pizzas for 6 people.

4. a. 8 boys:2 girls
b. $\frac{8}{10}$ of the students had seats.
c. $\frac{2}{10}$ of the students were girls.
d. 10 students:8 seats

5. a. Reporting a student to teacher ratio of 11:1 provides an index of how much attention a parent can expect his or her child to receive in the classroom.
b. The public school should hire 56 or 57 teachers. They could probably make the 11:1 claim if they had 56 teachers, but Because $624 \div 11 = 56$ R.8, they may hire 57.

6. a. You have a greater chance of winning with odds 6 for, 11 against than you do with odds of 3 for, 7 against.
b. 7(6:11) - 11(3:7) = (9:0)

7. a.

$\dfrac{27}{36}$  $\dfrac{20}{36}$

b. $\dfrac{3}{4} - \dfrac{5}{9} = \dfrac{27}{36} - \dfrac{20}{36} = \dfrac{7}{36}$

8. a.

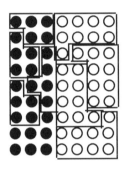

After removing 4 copies of 5:9, there were 7 extra dots, so 3:4 is greater.

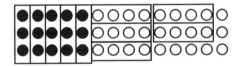

After removing 5 copies of 3:4, there were 7 "against" dots, so 5:9 is smaller.

b. 9(3:4) - 4(5:9) = (27:36) - (20:36) = (7:0)
   3(5:9) - 5(3:4) = (15:27) - (15:20) = (0:7)

9. Cloning 5:7 and removing copies of 8:11 we end up with 0:1, or 1 against. Thus, 8:11 is greater. 8(5:7)- 5(8:11) = 0:1

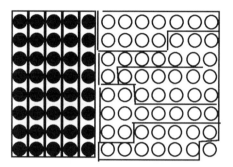

Cloning 8:11 and removing copies of 5:7, we end up with 1 for and 0 against, so 8:11 is greater. 7(8:11) - 11(5:7) = 1:0

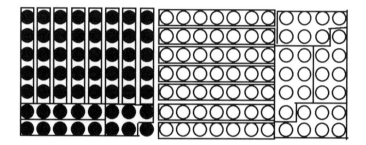

10. a. The second picture needs 5 circles. 6:15 = 2:5

b. The second picture needs 8 triangles. 2:5 = 8:20

c. The second picture needs 1 triangle. 6: 4 = $1\frac{1}{2}$: 1

11.

a.

$$\overset{\text{x100}}{\frown}$$

miles	$5\frac{3}{8}$	$500 + \frac{300}{8} = 537\frac{1}{2}$	$85 + \frac{51}{8} = 91\frac{3}{8}$	$537\frac{1}{2} + 91\frac{3}{8} = 628\frac{7}{8}$
days	1	100	17	117

x17

b.

cm.	2	4	1	.1	.6	4.6
km.	75	150	37.5	3.75	22.5	150 + 22.5 = 172.5

x2   ÷10   x6

÷2

c.

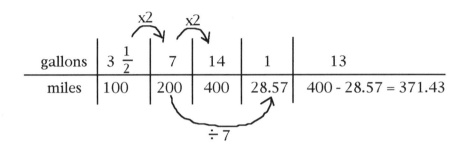

d.

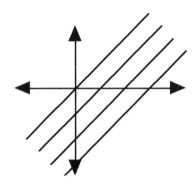

12. a. The difference is -4 for each pair.
b. y-x = -4

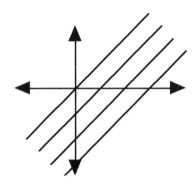

c. The lines are parallel. Each line has a slope of 1.
The difference is the y intercept or the point at which the line crosses the y axis.
d. The y coordinate is a multiple of the x coordinate. The ratio is 2:1.
e.

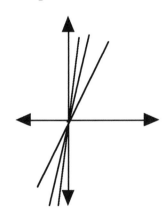

f. The lines all go through the origin and they all have different slopes. The ratio is the same as the slope.

g. Yes. There are many such lines. For example, draw the line through (0,3) and (2,4) and see that it does not go through (4,8).

h.   The line through (2,4) will also go through (4,8) if it also goes through the point (0,0).

i. The point (0,0) satisfies every equation of the form $y = mx$, where m is the slope of the line or the ratio y:x.

Chapter 12
Change

1. Time changed; distance from your starting point changed. Your speed remained constant for the three hours.

2. Time changed; the surface area of the balloon changed; the volume of the balloon changed; your puffing rate remained the same for one minute.

3. Time changed; your distance from home changed; your speed remained constant until you got to school.

4. Time changed; distance from the top of the hill changed; speed changed.

5. The cost increases for each subscription option because each involves a different period of time and a different number of magazines. However, if you analyze each option in terms of a 3-month rate, you can see that in each case, the 3-month subscription cost does not change. Six months costs 2($13.50); 9 months costs 3($13.50), and 12 months costs 4($13.50). Therefore, the same rate applies whether you buy the magazine for a shorter period of time or for a longer period of time.

6. a. The amount of water in the bathtub depends on how long the water has been running.
b How fresh your bread is depends on how many days have passed Because you baked it.
c. The amount of postage depends on the weight of your letter.
d. Your height depends on your age.

7. a. ↑↑ Three books should cost $17.40.
b. Correct. The time to walk to the mall does not depend on how many people are walking together.
c. You cannot correct this statement. People's weights do not work that way!
d. ↓↑ If fewer people work on the project, it will take more time to complete the project. It will take 5 people 8 weeks to do it.
e. ↓↓ It will take less time to write fewer invitations. It will take 24 minutes to write 6 invitations.
f. The time it takes to drive does not depend on how many people are in the car. It will still take one person 15 minutes to drive to the game.
g. The time it takes to swim a lap does not depend on how many people are swimming together.

8. a. periodic
b. decreasing
c. increasing
d. increasing
e. periodic
f. irregular

9. If you work 1 hour, you are paid $5.80. If you work 2 hours, you are paid $11.60. If you work 3 hours, you are paid $17.40. If you work 10 hours, you are paid 10 times as much as if you worked 1 hour. If you work a 40-hour week, you are paid 40 times as much as if you worked for 1 hour. This means that your work hours and your pay are increasing at the same speed.

10. One way you might begin to think about this is by making some assumptions. Assume that you start with a full tank of gas and that it takes exactly one tank of gas to reach your destination; decide how many miles per gallon you get in your car; and decide how many miles away your destination is. When you are a quarter of the way to your destination, half way to your destination, and three quarters of the way to your destination, do you have three quarters of tank of gas, half a tank of gas, and one quarter of a tank of gas, respectively, in your tank? You should find that, in fact, you do.

11. a. Graph #3 show the spread of the disease over time.
b. Graph #4 represents the distance Martha walked. Graph #2 could represent her velocity before she started to slow down.
c. Graph #2 shows ticket sales over time.
d. Graph #1 shows profits over time.
e. Graph #3 shows bacteria growth over time.
f. Graph #1 shows distance from the ground over time.
g. Graph #2 shows heat transfer over time. Graph #4 shows temperature of the pop over time.
h. Graph #1 shows distance over time.

12. a. This person ran for 15 seconds then turned around and ran back to the starting point.
b. This person ran at a steady pace for 30 seconds.
c. This person ran for 10 seconds, turned around and ran toward the starting point for 5 seconds, turned away from the starting point again and ran even faster for 5 seconds, then turned around and ran toward the starting point.

13.

a.   b.   c.

d.   e.   f.

g.   h.

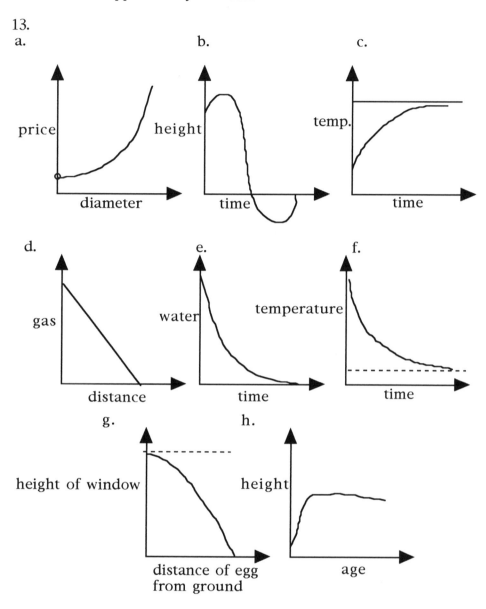

Chapter 13
Rates

1. a. 8 shaded: 12 unshaded
b. 4: 6
c. 2:3
d. 2:3, 4:4, and 8:12 are equivalent because the shaded and unshaded areas of the rectangle never changed. We merely renamed them by thinking of different-sized chunks.

e.

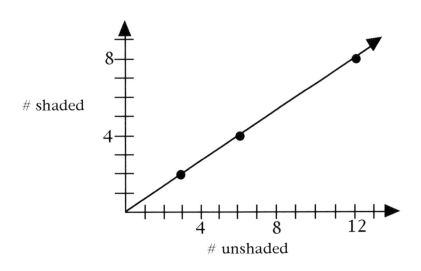

f. From any point on the line, draw a vertical line to the x axis and a horizontal line to the y axis to read its coordinates. Some that are easy to read from the graph are (3, 4.5), (5,7.5), (6,9), (7, 10.5)

g. The ratio of shaded to unshaded is the ratio of the y coordinate to the x coordinate. The ratios 7:3 and $1\frac{1}{2}:\frac{3}{4}$ are both greater than 1. 4:6 is on the line and 64:96 is on the line.

h. The constant is .667 (2 ÷ 3).

i. The slope of the line is the vertical change compared to the horizontal change between any tow point on the line. Using the points (3,2) and (6,4), we get $\frac{4-2}{6-3} = \frac{2}{3}$.

j.

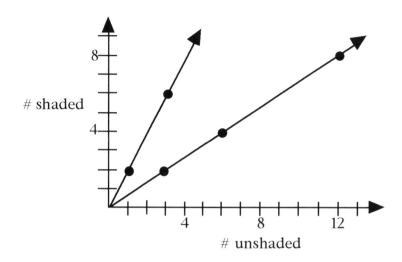

k. The constant associated with the class {2:1} is 2.

l.

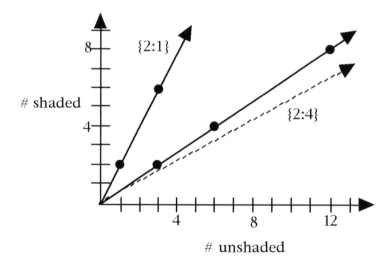

m. Judging by its slope, given by the unit ratio $= \frac{1}{2}$, the line is not as steep as either of the lines we have already graphed.

2. a. 30 heartbeats in 15 seconds is equivalent to 120 heartbeats per minute. 64 heartbeats in 30 seconds is equivalent to 128 heartbeats per minute. In the first case, the constant is 120, and in the second case, the constant is 128.

b. For a loss of 30 pounds in 7 months, the constant is 4.29. For a loss of 8 pounds in 6 weeks ($1\frac{1}{2}$ months), the constant is 5.33. The greater rate of loss is 8 pounds in $1\frac{1}{2}$ months.

3. a. In this graph, the steeper the line is, the more water the recipe contained in comparison to sugar. The steeper the line, the less sweet the mixture will taste. Recipe B represented by the line with the smallest slope will be the sweetest tasting.

b. Because all lines go through (0,0), a horizontal line would indicate that the recipe called for all sugar and no water.

4. a. 18°
b. 9° per hour (18 ÷ 2)
c. 18° is an absolute change and 9° per hour is a relative change. 9° per hour tells the change in temperature relative to the amount of time that elapsed during the time the temperature was dropping.
d. 6.5° per hour
e. 7.75° per hour (31 ÷ 4)
f. Each rate applies only to the interval for which it was calculated. The temperature was falling at different rates from 4—6 pm and from 6—8 pm. and the rate for the interval that combined these two rates will be different from both of them. For the 3 intervals, you will get three different rates unless the temperature was falling at a steady rate between 4 and 6 pm and between 6 and 8 pm. If, for example, the temperature had been falling at a rate of 6° per hour from 4 to 6 pm and at a rate of 6° per hour from 6 to 8 pm, the rate for the entire time period would also have been 6° per hour.

5. The quotient tells us that the average number of dollars spent on medical care per person was $1,900. It means that if we had distributed the total bill for medical care to every man, women, and child in the United States, each person would have to pay that amount.

6. a. $3 per pound is the same rate as $\frac{1}{3}$ pound per dollar. 3 pounds per dollar is the same rate as $.33 per pound.

b. 3 meters per second is the same rate as 1 meter in $\frac{1}{3}$ second, not 1 meter in 3 seconds.

7. Mark off a distance and measure it. Time how long it takes the boat to go that distance. Distance (if measured in meters) divided by time (minutes) will give you the speed of the current (meters per minute). You could then convert into km per hour.

8. We cannot tell who went farthest. To determine their distances, we need to know each person's rate and how long they were moving at that rate. Dennis' distance is the only one we know. He drove 110 miles.

9. One mile in 10 minutes = 1 mile in $\frac{1}{10}$ of a mile in a minute.

10. If the canoe floated down the river by itself, then its speed was the speed of the current because there was no rower. 7 miles in $1\frac{1}{2}$ hours = $4\frac{2}{3}$ mph (distance ÷ time = 7 mi. ÷ $\frac{3}{2}$ hr. = $4\frac{2}{3}$ mph).

11. Biking, the boy can travel 1 mile in 5 minutes ($\frac{1}{12}$ hour) or 12 mph. Walking, the boy can travel 1 mile in 20 minutes ($\frac{1}{3}$ hour) or 3 mph. To travel 8 miles to the office, it would take him $\frac{2}{3}$ hour to bike and $2\frac{2}{3}$ hours to walk. He could save 2 hours by biking.

12. a. An average of 5° per hour means that over the total time period, the temperature dropped 5° for each hour. So over 6 hours, the temperature dropped 30°.
b. We cannot tell how many degrees the temperature dropped during the first hour. An average temperature drop does gives us information about the total time period, but does not tell what happened each hour.

13. a. 110 miles in 3 hours = $36\frac{2}{3}$ mph.

b. 11 miles in 2.5 hours = $4\frac{2}{5}$ mph.

c. Average speed is 121 miles (110 + 11) ÷ 5.5 hours = 24.2 mph

14. Remember that distance one way is the same as distance the other way. If the biker went 10 mph for $\frac{1}{2}$ hour, then he traveled a distance of 5 miles. He walked back at the speed of 4 mph, so it must have taken him 5 mi. ÷ 4 mph or $1\frac{1}{4}$ hours to get back. Therefore, his total distance was 10 miles and his total time was $1\frac{3}{4}$ hours, giving an average speed of $10 ÷ 1\frac{3}{4} = 5\frac{5}{7}$ mph or 5.7 mph.

15. a. and b. Graph the given information. Because you know that you were driving a constant speed, you can extend the line between the two given points and see that 18 miles was the total distance and it took 22.5 minutes to drive it.

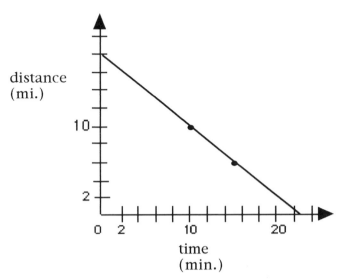

Algebraically, if x is the distance from the concert location to home, then 6(x - 10), the first distance divided by 10 min. or $\frac{1}{6}$ h r.) gives your speed and so does 4 (x - 6), the second distance divided by 15 min. or $\frac{1}{4}$ hour.

$$6(x - 10) = 4(x - 6)$$

$$x = 18 \text{ miles}$$

c. Your speed would be 18 miles ÷ $\frac{22.5}{60}$ hr. = 48 mph.

16.   Put time in seconds on the horizontal axis and distance on the vertical axis. Graph all four lines on the same graph. The points (3 min., 270 m) and (0,0) define the walking line; the points (3 min., 720 m) and (0,0) define the running line; the points (3 min., 210 m) and (0,0) define the swimming line; and the points (3 min., 162 m) and (0,0) define the crawling line. Draw a vertical line at the distance 300 m. and you will be able to read the approximate times corresponding to each type of locomotion. Running will take $1\frac{1}{4}$ minutes; walking, $3\frac{1}{3}$ minutes; swimming, $4\frac{1}{4}$ minutes; crawling, $5\frac{1}{2}$ minutes.

17. Carrie is 3 times as fast coming down as she is going up. This means that it must take her three times as long to go up as it takes her to come down. If you divide the total travel time of 6 hours by 4, you get 4 time periods of $1\frac{1}{2}$ hours each. It takes 3 time periods or $4\frac{1}{2}$ hours to go up. At the speed of $1\frac{1}{2}$ mph, the distance up is $1\frac{1}{2}$ mph $\cdot 4\frac{1}{2}$ hours = $6\frac{3}{4}$ miles.

18. Solving graphically, we can look for the point at which the boys' paths cross. Plot Ken's line through (0,0) and any other point given by his rate: $\frac{5 \text{ m}}{1 \text{ sec}} = \frac{15 \text{ m}}{3 \text{ sec}} = \frac{20\text{m}}{4 \text{ sec}}$ etc. Plot Jim's line starting at (30,0) and increasing at the rate of 3 meters for every second of the race. The lines intersect at a distance of 75 meters, 15 seconds into the race.

19. There is a change in sales of 70 pair when there is a change in price of $8. $\frac{70 \text{ pair}}{\$8}$ gives the rate of change of sales with respect to price.

20. The bus would have to come down the hill at a speed of 100 mph. if the average speed for the trip is to be 40 mph. Average speed = 40 mph = total distance (4 miles) ÷ total time (T). Then $T = \frac{4}{40} = .1$ hr. But at the speed of 25 mph on the way up, the 2 miles took .08 hr. That means that the time down has to be .1-.08 = .02 hr. The bus has to be 4 times as fast to come down in $\frac{1}{4}$ of the time it took to get up. It would have to come down at a speed of 100 mph!

Chapter 14
Reasoning Proportionally

1. a. Light reaching your book decreases as you move further from the bulb. Notice that when you move twice as far from the bulb, the intensity is $\frac{1}{4}$ what it was. If intensity and distance from the bulb were proportionally related, the intensity at 6 meters would be 60 units. This is not the case. In fact, intensity and (distance)^2 are inversely related.

b. By her first birthday, the baby would have grown 12 inches and would be about 33 inches tall—almost a yard. No! Growth is not proportionally related to time or age.

c. This situation does not involve any proportional or inversely proportional relationships. The number of A's in the class has nothing to do with how many people are in the class.

d. If the protozoa had a mass of 1 gram, after 8 hours, it would have a mass of 4 grams, after 12 hours, a mass of 8 grams. 12 hours is $1\frac{1}{4}$ times 8 hours, but 8 grams is twice 4 grams. The mass is increasing more rapidly than time is increasing. This is not a proportional relationship.

e. This situation does not involve any proportional or inversely proportional relationships. Spending more time studying does not always result in better grades.

f. The number of people is $\frac{2}{3}$ what it was, and when the number of people decreases, the time to do the work should increase. This situation involves an inversely proportional relationship between number of people and time it takes to do a job because the time was $\frac{3}{2}$ the time it took 3 people to do the work. $\frac{3}{2}$ of $1\frac{1}{4}$ is $\frac{15}{8}$, just under 2.

g. US dollars and British pounds are proportionally related because $3\frac{1}{3}$ as many dollars brought $3\frac{1}{3}$ times as many pounds.

h. Check the 3-month rate for each of the three prices given, and get $7.50 for 3 months. The length of subscription and cost are proportionally related.

i. If you make 50 phone calls, you pay $17.50. If you make 100 phone calls, you pay $22. The number of calls doubled, but the cost did not double. This is not a proportional relationship.

2.

a.

	meters	cost	notes
a	1	$2.99	given
b	5	14.95	5a
c	.1	.299	a÷10
d	.3	.897	3c
e	.01	.0299	c÷10
f	.07	.2093	7e
g	.001	.003	e÷10
h	.005	.015	5g
i	5.375	16.0713	b+d+f+h

$5\frac{3}{8}$ meters would cost $16.07.

b.

	pounds	price	notes
a	1	$1.29	given
b	5	6.45	5a
c	.1	.129	a÷10
d	.01	.0129	c÷10
e	.06	.0774	6d
f	5.16	6.6564	b+c+e

Six pounds would cost $6.66.

c.

	quotient	dividend	notes
a	1	36	given
b	10	360	10a
c	40	1440	4b
d	2	72	2a
e	42	1512	c+d
f	.1	3.6	a÷10
g	.7	25.2	7f
h	42.7	1537.20	e+g
i	.01	.36	f÷10
j	.02	.72	2i
k	42.72	1537.92	h+j
l	.001	.036	i÷10
m	.002	.072	2l
n	42.722	1537.992	k+m

The quotient rounded to hundredths is 42.72.

3. a. Not a proportional relationship.
b. $228.38.
c. .83 cup.
d. 27 boys.
e. Not a proportional relationship.
f. 25 hits.

4. a. Not a proportional relationship.

time (months)	cost (dollars)
6	18.80
9	28.00
12	37.00

$\times 2$ $\times 1.5$ $\times 1.49$ $\times 1.97$

b. Volume is proportional to area of base.

Area of Base (sq. in.)	Volume (cu. in.)
25	100
36	144
64	256

$\times 2.56$ $\times 1.44$ $\times 1.44$ $\times 2.56$

$V = 4A$

c. Not a proportional relationship.

# calls	charge
10	$13 + $.90 = $13.90
20	$13 + $1.80 = $14.80

$\times 10$ $\times 1.065$

5. Hold the weeks constant, and find out how many tubes 4 children would use in a week. Then hold the children constant and find out how many bottles they would use in 4 weeks.

children	6	3	1	4	4
tubes	1.5	.75	.25	1	4
weeks	1	1	1	1	4

6. Karl would be $6\frac{1}{4}$ steps high.

steps	5	2.5	1.25	6.25
bricks	8	4	2	10

7.

 a. They can decorate 12 cookies.   We can continue the table only until we use up one of the ingredients.

faces	1	10	2	12
j.b	3	30	6	36
M&M®	5	50	10	60

b. First, build a table so that it contains all four of the possible quantities.

faces	1	10	2	12	15	20	24
jb	3	30	6	36	(45)	60	(72)
M&M®	5	50	10	(60)	75	(100)	120

Then we can see that if he buys the bag of 45 jelly beans and the bag of 60 M&Ms®, he can decorate only 36 cookies and have 9 jellybeans left over. If he buys 72 jellybeans and 60 M&Ms®, he will have 36 jellybeans left over.   If he buys 45 jellybeans and 100 M&Ms® he can decorate 15 cookies and have 25 M&Ms® left over. If he buys 72 jellybeans and 100 M&Ms®, he can decorate 20 cookies and have 12 pieces of candy left over. John will probably buy 72 jellybeans and 60 M&Ms® .

8. We are told that the weight of statue A and its base = the weight of statue B and it base.

w(A) + w(base A) = w(B) + w(base B)

Substituting the other given information, we get:

2 w(base B) + w(base A) = 3w(base A) + w(base B)
Therefore, w(base B) = 2 w(base A).
Because w(A) = 2 w(base B), A must weigh 4 times the weight of its base.
B weighs 3 times the weight of base A.

So, A's weight is $\frac{4}{3}$ B's weight, and B's weight is $\frac{3}{4}$ A's weight.

9. a. There is an inverse proportional relationship between length of the lever and force required to do work. When the length of the lever is reduced to $\frac{1}{3}$ what it was, the force triples. We can express this relationship in the equation FL = 1890 or $F = \frac{1890}{L}$.

b. There is a proportional relationship between pounds recycled and the amount you are paid. The ratio of dollars to pounds = .40 or $\frac{\$.40}{1 \text{pound}}$. We can express this relationship with the equation d = .40 p.

c There is an inversely proportional relationship between volume of the gas and pressure. When the pressure increased to 1.3 times what it was, the volume of the gas was reduced to .77 times what it was. We can express this relationship with the equation PV = 16560 or $V = \frac{16560}{P}$.

10. When you buy 2 individual pints, each pint costs $.64, but when you buy a single 2-pint bottle of milk, the price per pint goes down $.60. When the number of pints doubled, the price did not double. Thus, the relationship between the number of pints and the cost is not proportional. We cannot predict the price of a gallon, nor can we predict the price of any other number of pints. All of the prices are not in the same class of relationships.

Chapter 15
Applications: Similarity and Percents

1. 12:9 = 4:3 = 8:6.

2. Congruent rectangles have the same dimensions. The ratios of their widths would be 1:1.

3.   One way to do this is to scale down using a scale factor whose denominator does not evenly divide 8 and 12. For example, using a scale factor of $\frac{1}{5}$, we get a rectangle whose dimensions are 1.6 x 2.4 units.

4. a.   By nesting the rectangles and drawing the diagonal, of the R rectangle, we can see that b, c, and d belong to the same family.
b. The ratio of the sides is 1.5 : 1.

5. We can determine the scale factor by comparing the bottom segments of the shape. From the smaller to the larger, this segment grew from 4 units to 10 units, thus increasing by a factor of 2.5.
Because the figures are similar, the other segments must increase by the same factor. 6 (2.5) = 15 units.

6.   a. When we enlarge the square, its length and width are both changed by the scale factor 3.
b.   The area, however, increases to 9 times the original area.

7. a. 10% of 80 = 8, 5% of 80 = 4, so 15% of 80 = 12
b. 5 = 10% of 50, 15 = 30% of 50
c. 10% of 70 = 7, 20% of 70 = 14
d. 21 is 50% of 42; 21 is 10% of 210; 21 is 5% of 420; 21 is 35% of 60
e. 27 is 50% of 54; 27 is 10% of 270; 27 is 5% of 540; 27 is 45% of 60

8. Marvin should buy the book at store C or store E. In either case, the book is half price.

9. Suppose the car cost $100. (Of course it does not, but we can use that amount to help think about the problem.) Then Mike sold the car to Kathy for $90. If Kathy gained 10% when she sold it back to him, she must have sold it for $99. In the end, Mike lost $9. $9 out of $100 is 9%. Mike had a 9% loss.

10.

a.

%	15	30	90	10	100
#	23	46	138	15.3333	153.3333

b.

%	36	72	18	90	10	100
#	42	84	21	105	11.66667	116.66667

c

%	100	50	10	30	5	35	.5	.1	.01	.03	35.13
#	74	37	7.4	22.2	3.7	25.9	.37	.074	.0074	.0222	25.9962

11. 35% off 39.99 is $14. Your total discount off the original price is $24. $24 is 48% of the original price.

Part IV
Challenging Problems

Part IV
Challenging Problems

Preservice teachers who are preparing for their preprofessional examinations may need some problems requiring computation. The following problems require both conceptual understanding and computational facility.

1. Roxie and her dad went on a hiking trip together on Morecrest Mountain. She carried the supplies $\frac{1}{3}$ of the way up and $\frac{3}{5}$ of the way down. If she carried the supply pack a distance of $17\frac{1}{2}$ miles, how far did they hike up the mountain?

2.

Here lies

Di O'Phantus

Before he ended his life, he composed this inscription so that you could figure out for yourself the age at which he died. He was a boy for 1/6 of his life, and 1/12 of his life later, became an adult. After 1/7 of this life, he married and 5 years later had a son. At only half his father's age, his son became ill and died. After trying to console himself for 4 years, Di ended his life.

3. In class yesterday, Professor Fracto noticed that $\frac{3}{4}$ of his students were female and there were 6 people absent. When he checked his records, he found that $\frac{2}{3}$ of those enrolled were female. Has there been a mistake?

4. A group of friends ate a bag of pistachios in one sitting, leaving just one nut in the bowl for me. They did not worry about dividing the nuts equally among themselves because they were too busy chatting and some like pistachios more than others do. Mandy took $\frac{2}{7}$ of them and Trish, $\frac{1}{12}$ of them. Alison and Kristen ate $\frac{1}{6}$ and $\frac{1}{3}$, respectively. Carol took 20, Kate took 12, and Pam, who was so busy talking that she forgot to eat, took 11 with her when she left. How many nuts were in the bowl before the girls got to them?

5. Solve this puzzle. It is time for bed! One fifth of three-eighths of what remains of the morning has already gone by. What time is it (to the nearest second)?

6. A man died and left to his elder son the task of splitting the five large bills, his lifetime savings. The son gave his brother twice two-thirds of his own share, and his mother $\frac{2}{8}$ of the younger brother's share. What fraction of the money did each receive?

7. Jim's wife had a baby yesterday morning. When the baby was born, the time until 12 noon was six times $\frac{2}{7}$ of the time since midnight. What time was the baby born?

8. Oscar, Harvey, and Merv each have huge collections of pennies. One day they decided to weigh them. Oscar discovered that his collection outweighed Harvey's by $\frac{1}{3}$ of Merv's. Harvey's was the weight of Merv's plus $\frac{1}{3}$ of Oscar's. Merv's collection weighed 10 pounds more than $\frac{1}{3}$ of Harvey's. How many pounds of pennies did each boy have?

9. Last Christmas, Mr. Moore gave each of his six daughters a box of a different weight, the lightest for the youngest, and so on until the heaviest went to the oldest. Each box was one ounce heavier than the next. If the sum of the weights was 6 pounds, what were the six weights?

10. A certain sculpture was made using 60 pounds of four different metals. The gold and bronze together accounted for $\frac{2}{3}$ of its weight. The gold and tin together comprised $\frac{3}{4}$ of its weight. The gold and iron together weighed 36 pounds. How much of each metal was used?

11. A man left this will.

I leave my son $\frac{1}{5}$ of my wealth, and my wife $\frac{1}{12}$. I leave to each of my four grandsons, my two brothers, and my grieving mother, $\frac{1}{11}$ of my property. To my cousins, I leave $12,000 to share and to my friend, Tom, $5,000. To my faithful employees I leave the following bonuses for their service: Ann, $350; Mark, $350; Steve, $600; Ray, $300; the delivery man, $200; the janitor, $200. It is my wish that $25,000 be spent on my mausoleum. Use $9,000 to cover the other costs associated with a modest funeral.

What was the dead man's fortune?

12. When my brother and I added the mileage we did on our bikes, we got 20 miles. If you add a third of my distance and a fourth of my brother's, you get 6 miles, the distance our mother cycled. How far did I go? How far did my brother go?

13. On Thursday night at the Larson household, each person gets home at a different time. Mike was home first. He skipped dinner, opened a bag of candy bars, and ate 6 of them. Alison came home next and helped herself to $\frac{1}{3}$ of the original contents of the bag. Mark got home just before Jenny and had $\frac{1}{2}$ of the remaining candy bars for his dessert. Jenny finished off the last two candy bars. Later, when Mrs. Larson got home and asked who ate the candy bars, Alison, the youngest, got blamed for eating most of the bag. For being so inconsiderate, she had to use her own money to buy a new bag of candy bars. Was this fair?

Solutions

1. Did you remember to ask yourself the most important question? What is the unit? The unit is the total distance Roxie and her dad walked. If Roxie carried the pack of supplies $\frac{1}{3}$ of the way up and $\frac{3}{5}$ of the way down, then she carried it $\frac{1}{3} + \frac{3}{5} = \frac{14}{15}$ of one way or $\frac{14}{30}$ of the total trip. Here is one way to picture the trip and Roxie's pack time.

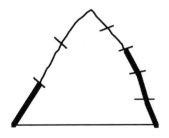

$17\frac{1}{2}$ miles is $\frac{14}{30}$ of the trip and $\frac{1}{30}$ of the trip is $1\frac{1}{4}$ miles, so $\frac{30}{30}$, the whole trip, must have been $37\frac{1}{2}$ miles. This means that Roxie and her dad hiked a distance of $18\frac{3}{4}$ miles up the mountain.

2. As you begin to work on Di O-Phantus' inscription, you find that the time until he became an adult was $\frac{1}{6} + \frac{1}{12}$ or $\frac{1}{4}$ of his life. The rest of the inscription describes $\frac{3}{4}$ of his life.

$$\frac{1}{6} + \frac{1}{12} + \frac{1}{7} + 5 \text{ years} + \frac{1}{2} + 4 \text{ years} = L$$

$$\frac{3}{4} + \frac{1}{7} + 9 \text{ years} = L$$

$$\frac{25}{28} + 9 \text{ years} = L$$

$$9 \text{ years} = \frac{3}{28} L$$

$$3 \text{ years} = \frac{1}{28} L$$

$\frac{28}{28}$ or his whole life must have been 84 years.

3. Clearly, the absent people cannot all be women (6 W, 0 M) because then it would be impossible that the number of women enrolled would be $\frac{1}{12}$ less than the number of women present. That leaves the following possibilities for the absent people:

Men	Women
1	5
2	4
3	3
4	2
5	1
6	0

The problems tells us that $\frac{3}{4}$ the number of women present (plus whatever women might be included in the absentees), is equal to $\frac{2}{3}$ of the enrolled students. If we let x be the number of students present in class, we can write this as $\frac{3}{4}x + (\text{absent women}) = \frac{2}{3}(x + 6)$.

Go through each case in the table. If the absent people were 1M,5W, we get $\frac{3}{4}x + 5 = \frac{2}{3}(x + 6)$. This is impossible because x, the number of people present turns out to be a negative number.

Next, if the absent people are 2M and 4W, solve the equation
$$\frac{3}{4}x + 4 = \frac{2}{3}(x + 6).$$

When you have exhausted all of the possible arrangements in the chart, you get the following possibilities:
There are 6 people enrolled. All 6 are absent. They are 2M, 4W.
There are 18 people enrolled. 12 are present. 3M, 3W are absent.
There are 30 people enrolled. 24 are present. 4M, 2W are absent.
There are 42 people enrolled. 36 are present. 5M, 1W are absent.
There are 54 people enrolled. 48 are present. 6M, 0W are absent.

4. The number of nuts in a full bag is $1 + \frac{2}{7}$ bag $+ \frac{1}{12}$ bag $+ \frac{1}{6}$ bag $+ \frac{1}{3}$ bag $+ 20 + 12 + 11$.

$\frac{2}{7}$ bag $+ \frac{1}{12}$ bag $+ \frac{1}{6}$ bag $+ \frac{1}{3}$ bag $= \frac{73}{84}$ bag, so 44 nuts must be $\frac{11}{84}$ bag.

4 nuts $= \frac{1}{84}$ bag and 336 nuts $= 1$ bag.

5. There are 12 hours of morning, so
what is past + what remains = 12 hours.
$\frac{1}{5}(\frac{3}{8}$ of what remains) + what remains = 12 hours.
Let R be the remaining part of the morning, then
$$\frac{3}{40}R + R = 12 \text{ hours}$$
$$1\frac{3}{40}R = 12 \text{ hours}$$
$$\frac{43}{40}R = 12 \text{ hours}$$
$$R = 11\frac{7}{43} \text{ hours}$$

So $\frac{36}{43}$ hour is gone. This is 50 minutes and 14 seconds.

6. The younger brother received $\frac{4}{3}$ the older brother's money and the mother received $\frac{1}{3}$ the older brother's money. If you let X = the amount the older brother kept, then $\frac{8}{3}X = 5$.

The older brother kept $1\frac{7}{8}$ of the bills.

The younger brother got $2\frac{1}{2}$ bills and their mother got $\frac{5}{8}$ of a bill.

7. The morning (12 hours total) is the time that the baby was born + the time that remained until noon. $x + \frac{12}{7}x = 12$. This means that the baby was born $4\frac{8}{19}$ hours into the morning, at 4:25 am.

8. If we let O stand for the weight of Oscar's collection, H, for the weight of Harvey's collection, and M, the weight of Merv's collection, then we get:

$$O = H + \frac{1}{3}M$$

$$H = M + \frac{1}{3}O$$

$$M = \frac{1}{3}H + 10$$

Substitute the expression for M and the expression for O into the second equation to get $H = \frac{1}{3}H + 10 + \frac{1}{3}H + \frac{1}{27}H + \frac{10}{9}$. Solve to get $H = 37\frac{1}{2}$ pounds, $O = 45$ pounds, and $M = 22\frac{1}{2}$ pounds.

9. If you let the first box weigh x oz, then the others weigh x+1, x + 2, x + 3, x+4, and x+ 5 ounces, respectively. Because the sum of their weights was 6 pounds, the first box weighed $13\frac{1}{2}$ ounces, and from that weight, you can get the others: $14\frac{1}{2}$ ounces, $15\frac{1}{2}$ ounces, 1 pound $\frac{1}{2}$ ounce, 1 pound $1\frac{1}{2}$ ounces, 1 pound $2\frac{1}{2}$ ounces.

10. You know that w(G) + w(B) + w(T) + w(I) = 60 and that
w(3G) + w(B) + w(T) + w(I) = 121.
The weight of 2 shares of gold must be 61.
G weighs $30\frac{1}{2}$ pounds, B weighs $9\frac{1}{2}$ pounds, T weighs $14\frac{1}{2}$ pounds, and I weighs $5\frac{1}{2}$ pounds.

11. The cash amounts mentioned in the will must be $\frac{53}{660}$ of the man's worth (W) because the fractional parts total $\frac{607}{660}$. So $53,000 = \frac{53}{660}$ W. W = $660,000.

12. Our mother went 6 miles, which was $\frac{1}{3}$ my distance $+ \frac{1}{4}$ my brother's distance. My brother's distance was (20 miles)-(my distance). Substituting that information into the mother's distance, you get that my distance was 12 miles. So my brother's was 8 miles.

13. What is the unit? This problem uses two different units. The number in the bag is the unit we ultimately want to determine. But, to get it, we first have to find out what unit was used to figure Mark's and Jenny's shares. The first unit we need refers to the number of candy bars remaining after Alison had her share. If Mark ate $\frac{1}{2}$ of the remaining candy bars, then $\frac{1}{2}$ of the remaining candy bars were left for Jenny. $\frac{1}{2}$ = 2 candy bars. The first unit, the number of candy bars remaining after Alison ate = 4 candy bars. Now determine the number of candy bars in the bag. We know that Alison ate $\frac{1}{3}$ of the candy bars in the bag, so the total eaten by everyone else must be $\frac{2}{3}$ of the bag.

$$6 + 2 + 2 = 10 \text{ candy bars or } \frac{2}{3} \text{ of the bag.}$$

If 10 bars = $\frac{2}{3}$ bag, then 5 bars = $\frac{1}{3}$ bag, and 15 candy bars = 1 full bag. Alison did not eat most of the bag. Mike did.